P9-BJW-561

MODERN IRAN

A Volume in the Comparative Societies Series

MODERN IRAN

A Volume in the Comparative Societies Series

GRANT FARR
Portland State University

HAROLD R. KERBO, Series Editor
California Polytechnic State University

QUEENS BOROUGH PUBLIC LIBRARY
INTERNATIONAL RESOURCE CENTER
FLUSHING BRANCH, 3RD FLOOR
41-17 MAIN STREET
FLUSHING, N.Y. 11355

 McGraw-Hill
College

Boston, Burr Ridge, IL Dubuque, Iowa Madison, WI
New York San Francisco, St. Louis
Bangkok Bogotá Caracas Lisbon London Madrid Mexico City
Milan New Delhi Seoul Singapore Sydney Taipei Toronto

McGraw-Hill College

A Division of The **McGraw·Hill** Companies

MODERN IRAN

Copyright © 1999 by The McGraw-Hill Companies, Inc. All rights reserved. Printed in the United States of America. Except as permitted under the United States Copyright Act of 1976, no part of this publication may be reproduced or distributed in any form or by any means, or stored in a data base or retrieval system, without the prior written permission of the publisher.

This book is printed on acid-free paper.

1 2 3 4 5 6 7 8 9 0 DOC/DOC 9 3 2 1 0 9 8

ISBN 0-07-292825-5

Editorial director: *Phillip A. Butcher*
Senior sponsoring editor: *Sally Constable*
Editorial coordinator: *Amy Smeltzley*
Marketing manager: *Leslie Kraham*
Project manager: *Kimberly D. Hooker*
Production supervisor: *Scott M. Hamilton*
Freelance design coordinator: *Laurie J. Entringer*
Compositor: *Shepherd, Inc.*
Typeface: *10/12 Palatino*
Printer: *R. R. Donnelley & Sons Company*

Library of Congress Cataloging-in-Publication Data

Farr, Grant M.
    Modern Iran / Grant Farr.
      p. cm.—(Comparative societies series)
    ISBN 0-07-292825-5
    Includes index
    1. Iran   I. Title.   II. Series
DS254.6.F37   1999
955—dc21
                                            98-26466

http://www.mhhe.com

This book is dedicated to my mother, Agnes Farr.

EDITOR'S PREFACE

In one of the early scenes of the movie *Reds*, the US revolutionary journalist John Reed, just back from covering the beginning of World War I, is asked by a roomful of business leaders, "What is this War really about?" John Reed stands, and stops all conversation with a one word reply—"profits." Today, war between major industrial nations would disrupt profits much more than create money for a military industrial complex. Highly integrated global markets and infrastructures support the daily life of suburban families in Chicago and urban squatter settlements in Bombay. These ties produce a social and economic ecology that transcends political and cultural boundaries.

The world is a very different place than it was for our parents and grandparents. Those rare epic events of world war certainly invaded their everyday lives and futures, but we now find that daily events thousands of miles away, in countries large and small, have a greater impact on North Americans than ever before, with the speed of this impact multiplied many times in recent decades. Our standard of living, jobs, and even prospects of living in a healthy environment have never before been so dependent on outside forces.

Yet, there is much evidence that North Americans have less easy access to good information about the outside world than even a few years ago. Since the end of the Cold War, newspaper and television coverage of events in other countries has dropped dramatically. It is difficult to put much blame on the mass media, however: international news seldom sells any more. There is simply less interest.

It is not surprising, then, that Americans know comparatively little about the outside world. A recent *Los Angeles Times* survey provides a good example: People in eight countries were asked five basic questions about current events of the day. Americans were dead last in their knowledge, trailing people from Canada, Mexico, England, France, Spain, Germany, and Italy.* It is also not surprising that the annual report published by the Swiss World Economic Forum always ranks American executives quite low in their international experience and understanding.

Such ignorance harms American competitiveness in the world economy in many ways. But there is much more. Seymour Martin Lipset put it nicely in one of his recent books: "Those who know only one country know no country" (Lipset 1996: 17). Considerable time spent in a foreign country is one of the best stimulants for a sociological

---

*For example, while only 3 percent of Germans missed all five questions, 37 percent of the Americans did (*Los Angeles Times*, March 16, 1994).

imagination: Studying or doing research in other countries makes us realize how much we really, in fact, have learned about our own society in the process. Seeing other social arrangements, ways of doing things, and foreign perspectives allows for far greater insight to the familiar, our own society. This is also to say that ignorance limits solutions to many of our own serious social problems. How many Americans, for example, are aware that levels of poverty are much lower in all other advanced nations and that the workable government services in those countries keep poverty low? Likewise, how many Americans are aware of alternative means of providing health care and quality education or reducing crime?

We can take heart in the fact that sociology in the United States has become more comparative in recent decades. A comparative approach, of course, was at the heart of classical European sociology during the 1800s. But as sociology was transported from Europe to the United States early in the 20th century, it lost much of this comparative focus. In recent years, sociology journals have published more comparative research. There are large data sets with samples from many countries around the world in research seeking general laws on issues such as the causes of social mobility or political violence, all very much in the tradition of Durkheim. But we also need much more of the old Max Weber. His was a qualitative historical and comparative perspective (Smelser 1976; Ragin and Zaret 1983). Weber's methodology provides a richer understanding of other societies, a greater recognition of the complexity of social, cultural, and historical forces shaping each society. Ahead of his time in many ways, C. Wright Mills was planning a qualitative comparative sociology of world regions just before his death in 1961 (Horowitz 1983: 324). [Too few American sociologists have yet to follow in his footsteps.]

Following these trends, sociology textbooks in the United States have also become more comparative in content in recent years. And while this tendency must be applauded, it is not enough. Typically there is an example from Japan here, another from Germany there, and so on haphazardly for a few countries in different subject areas as the writer's knowledge of these bits and pieces allows. What we need are the textbook equivalents of a richer Weberian comparative analysis, a qualitative comparative analysis of the social, cultural, and historical forces that have combined to make relatively unique societies around the world. It is this type of comparative material that can best help people in the United States overcome their lack of understanding about other countries and allow them to see their own society with much greater insight.

The Comparative Societies Series, of which this book is a part, has been designed as a small step in filling this need. We have currently selected 12 countries on which to focus: Japan, Thailand, Switzerland, Mexico, Eritrea, Hungary, Germany, China, India, Iran, Brazil, and Russia. We selected these countries as representatives of major world regions and cultures, and each will be examined in separate books written by talented sociologists. All of the basic sociological issues and topics will be covered: Each book will begin with a look at the important historical and geographical forces shaping the society, then turn to basic aspects of social organization and culture. From there each book will proceed to examine the political and economic institutions of the specific country, along with the social stratification, the family, religion, education, and finally urbanization, demography, social problems, and social change.

Although each volume in the Comparative Societies Series is of necessity brief to allow for use as supplementary readings in standard sociology courses, we have tried to assure that this brief coverage provides students with sufficient information to better understand each society, as well as their own. The ideal would be to transport every student to another country for a period of observation and learning. Realizing the unfortunate impracticality of this ideal, we hope to do the next best thing—to at least mentally move these students to a country very different from their own, provide something of the everyday reality of the people in these other countries, and demonstrate how the tools of sociological analysis can help them see these societies as well as their own with much greater understanding.

Harold R. Kerbo
San Luis Obispo, CA
June 1997

In 1979 Iran experienced a revolution that ranks among the most important and profound in world history. Millions of Iranians took to the
streets in the cities and towns of Iran willing, it seemed, to give their
lives in the effort to overthrow the Shah of Iran and his ruling oligarchy.
The Iranian people, mostly unarmed, were able to drive the Shah of Iran
from power. Iranian society was turned upside down and profoundly
transformed. The religious clergy, with the Ayatollah Khomeini at the
head, established an Islamic government, which appeared to bring back
an older form of religious rule but which, in fact, created a kind of political Islam that the Islamic world had not seen before.

The United States and Iran have become bitter enemies in the aftermath of that revolution. Americans continue to view Iranians and Iran in
a negative light. In 1979 Iranian youth stormed the American Embassy in
Tehran and held American diplomats hostage for more than one year.
Each night during the hostage crisis American television showed the
American viewing public tens of thousands of Iranians demonstrating at
the US Embassy in Tehran chanting, "Death to America." It was a time of
great emotion and anger in both the United States and Iran. Eight American servicemen lost their lives, and many Iranians in the United States
were insulted or mistreated.

In the aftermath of the Islamic revolution of 1979, the Iranian leaders told their people that everything from the United States, and the
West in general, was bad. America was, and still is, referred to as the
"Great Satan" (the former Soviet Union is the "Little Satan"). Iranian
leaders continue to this day to preach of the evils of American life and
society. Almost 20 years after the Iranian revolution, the United States
and Iran still do not have diplomatic relations, and the rhetoric of distrust and hatred continues on both sides. To many Americans, Iran still
appears to be a country of religious fanatics, troublemakers, terrorists,
and religious zealots—traditionalist, bearded, and anti-Western.

Yet there is another side to this story. Historically, there have been
good relations between the United States and Iran, and between Americans
and Iranians. Thousands of Iranian university students have studied in the
United States, and over a quarter million Iranians now live in the United
States, most, but not all, of whom came to the United States after the revolution. Over the years, many Americans, including this author, have
worked and traveled in Iran. Americans have generally been well treated
and graciously accepted in Iran, even during the Islamic revolution.

While the West now thinks of Iran as a country of violence and fa-
naticism, it is also a society that has produced great poetry and beautiful

literature, a society of enlightened philosophers and learned scholars. It is a country of great buildings and beautiful gardens and parks. Iranians are gracious hosts. Anyone invited to an Iranian's home will be treated with great respect and courtesy. Iranian society also values many of the same things American society values, appearances aside. In Iran the family and community are important. In sum, Iranians are gracious, cultured, and enlightened people, with a long tradition of culture and history.

In fact, as this book will show, we in the West know very little about Iran. Iran is vitally important to the West, if for no other reason than that it has enormous oil reserves, yet we know very little about who the Iranians are, their history and culture, the way their society works, and how they see the world. As we will find out, even though Iranians geographically are part of the Middle East, their cultural background is not Arabic or Turkish, as is most of the Middle East. While Iran shares much with other countries around it, it is also unique, with its own particular way of doing things. In fact, Iran has more in common with the West than we appear to know.

The challenge of this book is to understand both sides of this paradox. To do this, we will examine Iran from several points of view. This examination will use the tools of sociology to look at Iranian society. How does their social structure work, how do the Iranians see the world, and what is important in their society? We will find that to understand Iran, we must know something of its history and geography. Iran has a long and colorful history that goes back for over three thousand years. Iranians know their historical heritage and are proud of it.

This examination of Iran will also look at Iranian geology and geography. The mountains, plains, and deserts of Iran play an important role in shaping Iranian society, just as the geography of the United States has played an important role in the shaping of American society. In addition, it will be important to look at the location of Iran in the world. Between east and west, and between north and south, Iran's central position in the crossroads between Europe and Asia has allowed it to play an important political and economic role in the region, but has also opened it to attack from marauding armies.

We will also look at some of the important social institutions in Iran. What is the role of the family in Iran, and is it different from the role of the family in the United States? How do Iranians find a mate, get married, raise their children, and treat their elderly? Are the roles and expectations of women and men different in Iran than in the West, and why is this?

We will also examine the role of religion. The religion of Islam plays a very important role in Iranian society, perhaps a more important role than religion plays in American society. But what are the basic tenets of Islam, and how are they different from the basic tenets of other religions, especially Judaism and Christianity, to which it is closely related? And how is Islam interpreted in the daily life of the average Iranian?

To solve this paradox of the two Irans, we will also look at social inequality in Iran. Are there social classes in Iran, and if so, how many and how are they determined? Can individuals improve their position in the Iranian social stratification system? How? And probably of more importance, what are the consequences of being upper or lower class?

We will also examine the demographic characteristics of Iran. We will see that Iranian society is growing rapidly. It has a high birth rate and declining death rate. Why is this, and what are the consequences for Iranian society? An examination of the cities of Iran is also of importance. Cities of the Middle East, including Iran, existed much earlier than those in Europe and the United States. In addition, cities in Iran are growing rapidly not just from the high birth rate, but also because people are leaving the countryside and moving into the urban areas. Iranian cities are becoming crowded and lack proper services.

Finally we must see Iran in the bigger picture, that is, in its relations to its neighbors and the other countries of the world. Iran is part of the world system of countries. It is embedded in a series of concentric webs of obligations and rights with other countries and peoples. Starting from the smallest web, Iran is the center of Persian culture. Other Persian-speaking countries in the surrounding area, including Afghanistan, Tajikastan, and parts of Uzbekistan look to Iran as the heartland of Persian language and literature.

Iran is also an Islamic country and shares with other Islamic countries obligations to the rituals and duties of the Islamic faith. These Islamic obligations include the pilgrimage to Mecca and the care of important Islamic shrines, as well as political and economic support for Islamic movements around the world.

Iran is also located in the area of the world now called the Middle East. Although culturally distinct from other Middle Easterners like the Turks, Arabs, or Israelis, Iranians nonetheless share much in common with their neighbors in the region. Iran belongs to OPEC, the Organization of Petroleum Exporting Countries, for instance, and is an important oil-producing nation.

Finally, Iran is a significant country in the world of nations. It belongs to the United Nations and has economic, political, and cultural relations with many countries. Despite the economic ban placed on Iran by the United States, Iran trades actively with most of the European nations and Japan. It has close ties with China and Russia, as well with other countries in the region, particularly Pakistan. Historically, Iran was never colonized by the West, as were many of the other Middle Eastern countries, but nonetheless its development was clearly shaped by its association with the Western powers.

I would like to express my gratitude to my wife Mary Ellen Page Farr, for her help on this manuscript, and to my colleagues Professor Veronica Dujon, Lee Haggerty, Arezu Movahed, Robert Liebman, and Robert Shotola. These dear friends suffered my tedious chatter about this book and listened kindly, and their suggestions have helped immensely. My greatest gratitude goes to Professor Leonard Cain. Dr. Cain patiently read every word of this manuscript, correcting or questioning every strange usage, every misspelling, and every misplaced comma. He helped me enormously, and I am a better writer because of him.

There are two technical points to make. First, there is no agreed-upon transliteration of Persian words into English. Therefore, I have tried to use the most common English spellings of the Persian or Arabic words so that readers who might see the words elsewhere would recognize them. My apologies to the linguistic purists. Second, when written by Moslems, the name of the Prophet Mohammed is followed by a salutation, generally "peace be upon him." For editorial efficiency I have not done this. I mean no disrespect to the Islamic religion.

Finally, I write this book with deep affection and profound respect for the Iranian people. I have lived and traveled in Iran for many years and was a professor at an Iranian university. I have almost always been treated with the greatest respect, courtesy, and hospitality in Iran, even by strangers who did not know me. I continue to have friends in the Iranian community, both in Iran and in the United States.

Iran is a complex society, and I would never claim to understand it completely. I have tried to be fair to all sides of the Iranian story and to describe and analyze the situation in Iran honestly and objectively. Iranians are wonderful people, and they deserve to have their story told.

Grant Farr

CONTENTS

Chapter 3

Family, Marriage, and Kinship   31

Chapter 4

Religion in Everyday Life   40

Chapter 5

The Iranian Political System   55

Chapter 9

Population and Urbanization   99

Chapter 10

Social Change in Iran   113

MODERN IRAN

A Volume in the Comparative Societies Series

MODERN IRAN

A Volume in the Comparative
Societies Series

CHAPTER 1

Iranian Society and Its Environment

INTRODUCTION: THE STORY

Each society in the world has its own story. The story tells about the society, who its people are, how and where they live, and how they feel and think. Each story is unique, yet there is often a common thread that runs through these stories. Iranian society is much like this. Its story is unique. It has a special history and place in the world. It is like no other country. But despite its uniqueness, Iran also has much in common with other countries in the world, including the United States. Unfortunately, in the last few decades, the story of Iran has not been a pleasant one, at least in the Western world. Iran has come to be viewed as a terrorist state, a country of religious fanatics. Iranian culture has seemingly rejected everything Western and turned in a different direction. The United States is called the "Great Satan" in Iran. Even now, 20 years after the Islamic revolution that transformed Iran, there are no diplomatic ties between the United States and Iran.

Yet there is another part of the Iranian story that is unfortunately largely unknown in the Western world. This is the story of a country of great poetry and literature, of an enlightened society with important philosophers and learned scholars. Another part of the story not heard in the West is of an Iran that values family ties and views community obligations as critical to the well-being of the society, where neighbors watch out for each other in traditional neighborhoods, and where the elderly are cared for in the family setting. This story of Iran includes a culture that values graciousness and hospitality and a society in which guests are treated like royalty.

Our task then is to learn the whole story of Iran—the good and the bad. This chapter begins this assignment by examining who the Iranians are, what their country is like, and where it is located. Part of the Iranian story is influenced by its location in the world. Because of its location, particularly its position between Asia and Europe, Iran has been a player in world history for thousands of years. The story must also include an understanding of Iran's geographical characteristics. The deserts, mountains, plateaus, and coastlines of Iran are as important in determining who the Iranians are as the geography of America is in shaping who Americans are. The story of Iran is also built upon its cultural diversity. Iran includes many ethnic groups, several languages, and people of different physical features.

Before beginning the story of the Iranian people, a few definitions are in order. In current usage, the modern country is called **Iran,** or more completely the **Islamic Republic of Iran** (in Persian, *Jomhuri-e Islami-e Iran*). The language most Iranians speak is Persian, and the country was called Persia by most of the outside world until the 1930s, although the Iranians themselves have always referred to their country as Iran. The people of Iran can be called Iranians, referring to their modern citizenship, or Persians, referring to their culture and language, although many Iranians speak other languages besides Persian. Both words—"Iran" and "Persia"—have ancient origins. Iran, or Iranian, connotes ties to the ancient Aryan culture that settled on the Iranian plateau thousands of years ago. The words "Iran" and "Aryan" are cognates. "Persian" refers to the people of the Fars, a province in Southern Iran and an important location of early Iranian historical developments. The Persian language is called *Farsi* in Persian. The "P" was changed to "F" by the Arabs, who do not have a "P" sound in their alphabet. The Ancient Greeks used the older pronunciation, and so they called these people *Persian*. The name has stuck.

THE LOCATION

Like many countries, Iran's location and physical characteristics have been important in shaping its culture and the nature of its society. Iran is located in the part of the world generally called the Middle East, although it should be noted that the term *Middle East* is of Western etymology, originally used to distinguish between the European interests in the Near East and the Far East. The world region that includes Iran is sometimes also called Southwest Asia or the Gulf Region. (The gulf that borders Iran on the south is called the *Persian* Gulf in Iran and the *Arabian* Gulf in the Arab countries.) The Middle East, as it is now thought of, is composed of about 25 countries and includes North Africa, the eastern end of the Mediterranean, the countries of the Saudi Arabian peninsula, Turkey, and Iran. Since this definition is somewhat arbitrary, other countries such as Afghanistan and parts of Central Asia are sometimes included in the Middle East. The Middle Eastern countries are mainly Arabic speaking, except for Turkey, Iran, and Israel, and typically Islamic, except for Israel (Keddie, 1973).

Iran is strategically positioned with Iraq and Turkey on its western border, Afghanistan and Pakistan on its eastern border, and the Newly Independent States of Armenia, Azarbaijan, and Turkmenistan on its northern border. Iran has a considerable coastline, including 2,440 km along the important Gulf of Oman and the Persian Gulf, which demar-cates its southern border, and 749 km of coastline along the Caspian Sea to the north.

The total area of Iran is 1.648 million square kilometers. Iran is the 16th largest country in the world, about one-fifth the size of the continental United States; that is, slightly larger than Alaska (Metz, 1987).

Iran's central location at the crossroads of Europe and Asia has had an important impact on its history. Unlike other countries that are tucked out of harm's way, Iran is on the main route from South Asia to Europe, and on the main route from Central Asia to the Persian Gulf. This central location has put Iran in the center of international trade and commerce. Before the advent of modern sea transport, Iran was on the famous Silk Road, which connected Europe with China between the second century and eighth century AD. During World War II Iran was a main route by which the Allies supplied Russia. Now it is becoming an important bridge connecting the newly emerging countries of Central Asia to the West, particularly for the shipment of Central Asian oil.

Iran's central location has also put it directly in the path of conquer-ing armies as well. Iran has been invaded over its long history by Alexander the Great, the Arabs, the Turks, the Mongols of Genghis Khan, and more recently the Russians and the British, although the Rus-sians and British never actually occupied Iran. All of these invasions have left their mark on Iranian culture and society.

THE PLACE

The physical features of a country determine many of its social and eco-nomic characteristics. Iran is a land of contrast. It is one of the most mountainous countries in the Middle East, yet it is an arid country with deserts and dry plains, but also in the north along the Caspian Sea it has a fertile plain. Essentially Iran is like a bowl: mountains surrounding a high basin. In the center of the bowl is the Central Plateau composed of deserts and semi-arid plains. Unlike the great sand deserts in other areas of the Middle East, such as the Sahara or Arabian deserts, which can sup-port some human life, the Iranian deserts are completely uninhabitable places, in many areas covered with salt or rocky ground. The two main deserts are the *Dasht-e Lut* and the salt desert *Dasht-e Kavir*, both in cen-tral and eastern Iran.

Around the edges of the bowl are two large mountain ranges, the Elburz Mountains in the north and the Zagros Mountains in the south. The Zagros Mountains are higher and larger than the Elburz, with sev-eral peaks above 4,000 meters. However, the highest peak in Iran is Mount Damavand, which is in the Elburz Range just north of Tehran. Mount Damavand is 5,600 meters high, the highest mountain in the Eurasian landmass west of the Hindu Kush. On the slopes of these mountains, particularly the Zagros, pastoral nomads move their flocks into the high pastures in the heat of summer and down onto the plains in the cool of winter. The number of pastoral nomads has decreased in Iran in the last several decades, partly because of the policies of recent Iran governments to settle them, but also because pastoral nomadic life clashes with modernization. However, pastoral nomads, with their distinctive way of life and strong kin structure, have played an important role in Iranian culture and history.

The center of this bowl is closed. There are no major river systems into or out of the Iranian Central Plateau. The water from the mountains drains into the arid plains, where it evaporates or empties into barren salt lakes. Rivers and stream beds fill during the spring snow melt but are dry for much of the year. There are a few smaller rivers on the periphery of Iran that drain away from the Central Plateau into the Caspian Sea in the north or the Persian Gulf in the south. Because there are no major internal river systems, water travel did not develop in Iran. Traditionally, the Iranians have depended on overland travel, by camel caravans in the past and, in modern times, by truck or bus. There is a train system in Iran, but its use has been limited.

The climate in Iran is generally hot and dry, particularly in the south, with temperatures over 90° F for much of the summer. Rain, especially on the Central Plateau, is scarce, below five inches a year over much of the area, making farming without irrigation impossible. In the mountains, however, there are greater amounts of rain, and snow in the winter at higher elevations. The north of Iran is colder. In fact, winters in Tehran and in the northern cities such as Tabriz are cold, with ice and snow and temperatures below freezing much of the winter months. In the winter months there is skiing in the mountains just north of Tehran.

Along the Persian Gulf, in the southwest corner of Iran, in the area called Khuzestan, the weather is very hot and humid, often reaching 100° F or hotter during the summer months. In this part of Iran, most outdoor activities in the summer months cease during the hot hours of the day. Even government offices and the universities in this area shut during the hot afternoons. Traditional homes in this area are constructed to accommodate the extreme temperatures and humidity. Large areas of Khuzestan are uninhabitable salt marshes, especially near the confluence of the Tigris and Euphrates rivers.

In the narrow lateral between the Elburz Mountains and the Caspian Sea, rainfall is much greater, over 30 inches annually in some places, making possible the growing of crops that need a great deal of water, especially tea. This green belt offers a stark contrast to the hot and dry climate of the rest of the country, and many Iranians travel to this area for a cool break from the heat and dust of the typical Iranian summers.

POPULATION

The population of Iran was estimated to be over 67 million in 1997 (US Bureau of the Census, 1997), making it one of the most populous nations in the Middle East. (There is some contention regarding the size of Iran's current population. Some estimates have it somewhat lower. The difficulty of estimating populations in countries such as Iran will be discussed in the chapter on population trends, Chapter 9.) Most of Iran's rapid population growth is because it has a high fertility rate; approximately 4.5 children were born per woman in 1997 (US Bureau of the Census, 1997). As a result of this high fertility rate, a high percentage, about 45 percent, of the population is under the age of 15, creating an enormous burden on the country.

Iran also has a relatively high infant mortality rate. Approximately 52 babies out of 1,000 born die each year before reaching the age of one (World Factbook, 1997). More will be said about the population dynamics of Iran later in the book, especially regarding the family planning attitudes of the Islamic government, the value of large families in Iranian society, and the social problems created by such a large percent of the population under 15 years of age.

The largest city and capital of Iran is Tehran, with a population close to 12 million. Tehran is now the 16th largest urban area in the world, larger, for instance, than London. Tehran is also one of the world's more dense cities, at 33,726 people per square kilometer (World Urban Areas, 1991). There are other important cities in Iran, including Mashad (1,419,000), in the northeastern corner of Iran near the Afghan border; Isfahan (928,000), in the center of the country; Tabriz (808,000), in the northwest; and Shiraz (800,000), the capital of Fars province in the southern area (1986 Iranian National Census). While Tehran itself is a relatively new city, many of the cities of Iran have ancient roots and rich historical pasts.

THE PEOPLE

Although Iranians are a mixture of several different cultures, physically they are of the type that is often referred to as Mediterranean, as are most of the people in the Middle East. The exceptions are in the northeast of Iran near the border with Turkmenistan, where the people take on the physical characteristics of Central Asians with pronounced Mongoloid features, and along the area of the Persian Gulf lateral, where Arab and Eastern African influences can be seen.

In Iran, physical appearance, or what is often called *race* in the West, is not an important marker of social status. Therefore, racial prejudice and discrimination are not important social issues in Iran as they are in the United States. This does not mean that Iran is free of prejudice and discrimination, but that other social distinctions, such as kin group or religious sect, are more important status markers in Iran than is physical type. In addition, there is less variation in physical type in Iran than there is in the United States. There is, therefore, less opportunity for racism when most people look alike. Finally, racial discrimination is not seen in Iran, because the groups that are physically different tend to live in isolated corners of Iran, along the Persian Gulf, for instance, or in the northeast corner near the border with Turkmenistan, and are generally not part of the national culture.

LANGUAGE

While several languages are spoken in Iran, Persian is the official language. It is the language of public education and of government, and the native language of over half of the population, mostly those who live on the Iranian Central Plateau. Most Iranians can speak Persian, at least as a second language, since most education, business, media, and government bureaucracies work in Persian. While other languages are widely spoken in some areas of Iran in nongovernmental and domestic settings, the use of non-Persian vernacular languages in schools or newspapers has largely been forbidden.

As in most countries, there are strong regional dialects of Persian, so people from various areas of Iran can easily be identified by their accent.* Some dialects of Persian are so different that they are hardly understandable to Persian speakers from other areas.

Persian is an ancient language that developed over a long period of time. Modern Persian surfaced in Iran in the ninth century after a period during which Arabic had been the official language. As a consequence, modern Persian has been strongly influenced by Arabic. To this day Persian is written in Arabic script and contains many Arabic loan words. For several centuries Iranian scholars have tried to eliminate, or at least diminish, the influence of Arabic on Persian, particularly the use of Arabic words in the Persian vocabulary, largely to no avail. In the 1930s, Reza Shah, the leader of Iran at that time, even considered Romanizing the writing of Persian, as Ataturk had done with Turkish, so as to further diminish the influence of Arabic on the language. Since the Islamic revolution in 1979, however, the use of Arabic words and sayings in Iran has increased, mostly because Arabic is the liturgical language of the Islamic religion and most of the religious leaders in Iran are fluent in Arabic.

Persian is a member of the Indo-European language family, and, therefore, related to most of the European languages, including English, but not to the other major languages in the Middle East, Arabic and Turkish. As a result, Persian is relatively easy for English speakers to learn, as compared with, say, Arabic, because it has a similar logic and syntax. It is also a language of consistent grammatical rules, unlike English. Verb conjugations are regular with few exceptions, the rules for the formation of plurals are straightforward, sentence order is uniform and

---

*Author's Note: I originally learned to speak Persian while in the Peace Corps in Afghanistan. In Afghanistan, the Persian language is called *Dari*, and, while generally understood by Iranians, has some major differences in pronunciation and grammar. As a result, when I speak in Persian with Iranians, they can generally tell that I learned Persian in Afghanistan, which they regard as amusing.

consistent, and Persian does not make gender distinctions in nouns or articles. The challenge for English speakers trying to learn Persian is to master the Arabic script, to learn to vocalize some of the sounds unfamiliar to English speakers, and to master the extensive Persian vocabulary. In addition, Persian, unlike American English, makes distinctions between polite and casual conversation. When speaking in Persian, one must be aware of whether the person to whom one is speaking is more important or less important, younger or older, and so on.

The significance of the Persian language in Iran is not only in its historical importance, but also in its role as a literary language. Iranians, and others, consider spoken Persian to be beautiful and take pleasure in listening to the recitation of the poems of the major medieval poets such as Ferdowsi, Hafiz, and Sadi. Poetry is an important source of literary expression, and many Iranians know the great poems of their language by heart. To many Iranians, modern Persian is an important link to their country's past, and the language provides a vital cultural commonality that binds the country together.

In addition, over the centuries Iran has had a strong culture and social presence in the adjoining regions so that Persian has been adopted as a classical language of many of the surrounding cultures. Over 100 million people presently speak Persian, or one of its dialects. In Pakistan, for instance, Persian was taught until the 1930s as an important cultural language, much like Latin was taught in Europe and the United States. Because Persian was considered to be such a beautiful language, Pakistani and Indian poets wrote in Persian, as did Ottoman poets in Turkey at one time. It was the official language of India during the Mughal period in the 18th century until Urdu replaced it as the official language of India in 1837 (Spooner, 1992). Persian is one of the two official languages of Afghanistan, where it is also widely spoken and referred to as Dari. Persian is also spoken in several countries of Central Asia, particularly in Tajikistan, where it is called Tajik and written in the Cyrillic script. There are strong dialectical differences in these variants of Persian, although a speaker of one of these dialects can usually understand speakers of another.

Iran is considered the heartland of the Persian language, and the Persian speakers in the surrounding countries look toward Iran as the center of Persian culture. In the last several decades with the advent of modern media, especially radio and TV, the Tehran dialect has come to dominate spoken Persian. As a result, most teachers of Persian at American universities teach Tehran Persian.

Iran is also composed of other ethno-linguistic groups. As Table 1–1 shows, only 58 percent of Iranians are native Persian speakers. Over one-quarter of the people in Iran speak a Turkic language as their mother tongue, mostly Azarbaijani, also called Azari, the language of Azarbaijan. The Azarbaijanis live in the prosperous northwest area of the country near the Turkish border and the newly independent country of Azarbaijan. Azarbaijani is similar to the Turkish spoken in Turkey and

TABLE 1−1

Language Groups in Iran

Persian and Persian dialects	58%
Turkic and Turkic dialects	26
Kurdish	9
Luri	2
Baloch	1
Arabic	1
Others	3

Source: Based on information from Metz, 1987.

related to many of the languages of Central Asia such as Uzbek, Kyrgyz, and Kazakh. The Iranian city of Tabriz is the center of Azarbaijani culture in Iran, and most of the population of Tabriz speak Azarbaijani as their mother tongue. Because of their success in business, Azarbaijanis have spread throughout Iran, and there are sizable communities of Azarbaijanis in most Iranian cities. It is estimated that one-third of the population of Tehran is Azarbaijani, for instance (Metz, 1987).

Azarbaijanis are largely urban dwellers, and their lifestyle is similar to that of the Persians. Although Azarbaijanis are sometimes the butt of ethnic jokes, they are generally well integrated into Iranian culture, and many hold high positions in the government and are successful in business and other areas of life. A number of important religious leaders, for instance, are Azarbaijanis. Intermarriage with Persians is common among the middle and upper classes in the urban areas. Most educated Azarbaijanis are bilingual in Persian.

Other languages as well are spoken in Iran, including Kurdish, also an Indo-European language related to Persian, and Arabic, in the Semitic language family.

As a result of this linguistic mix, most Iranians who are not native Persian speakers are bilingual by necessity, or for that matter, multilingual, speaking Persian at their work or while dealing with the official culture, but speaking their native language at home. Unlike Americans, most Iranians accept that there are several languages spoken in their country and that they must become bilingual to be successful.

Iran has been able to maintain a strong national identity despite the multiethnic mix. With some exceptions, most people in Iran generally identify themselves as Iranians, despite differences in native language or ethnicity, and participate in the national culture. Secessionist movements have occurred, but they have been relatively rare given the diverse nature of the Iranian population. The major exception is among the Kurds, who live in the northwest corner of Iran near the Turkish and Iraqi borders. The Kurds have generally resisted assimilation into Iranian life and have remained attached to Kurdish nationalistic movements in Turkey and Iraq whose goal it is to create a Kurdish nation.

RELIGIONS

Moslems

Iranians are overwhelmingly Moslems, following the branch of Islam referred to as Shia Islam. Some definitions are needed. Both the words *Islam* and *Moslem* (and the word used in greeting, *salam*) derive from the Arabic root meaning submission, as in submission to God's will. "Islam" refers to the religion that God revealed to the Prophet Mohammed and "Moslem" to the people of Islam. Moslems do not refer to their religion as Mohammedism, as it has sometimes been called in the West, as Christians refer to their religion as Christianity, meaning the religion of Christ. Rather, Moslems believe that Mohammed was a prophet of God, and a messenger of God's word, but not the son of God, and therefore to call the religion Mohammedism would be incorrect.

Most Moslems in the world follow a branch of Islam referred to as Sunni Islam. Shia Islam, as practiced in Iran, is different than Sunni Islam. Shia Islam believes that after Mohammed's death in AD 632, the line of succession to the leadership of Islam passed to Ali, Mohammed's son-in-law, and subsequently to Ali's male descendants. Shias refer to Ali and the spiritual leaders of Shia Islam who followed him as *Imams,* meaning the spiritual leader of the Islamic community. Most Moslems do not accept this Shi'ite view, arguing that the next leader of Islam after Mohammed should have been Abu Bakr. The debate over the leadership of the Islamic community after the Prophet Mohammed created a split in the Islamic community in the first three centuries of Islam, and the Sunni view has prevailed in much of Islam.

Among the Shia Moslems there are several sects. The branch of Shia Islam that dominates Iran follows the descendants of Ali through 12 *Imams,* counting Ali, at which time the line of *Imams* ceases. The followers of this version of Shi'ism are therefore sometimes called the Twelvers (*ithna-ashari*). This Twelver form of Shia Islam is also found in Bahrain, Iraq, and Lebanon. More will be said about the tenets of Shi'ism and its role in Iranian society in the chapter on religion.

While Shia Islam of the Twelver variety dominates Iran, other branches of Islam are found in the country. Most of the ethnic Arabs, Kurds, and Baloch in Iran are Sunnis, for instance, making up about 10 percent of the population. The Shia recognize the Sunni as fellow Moslems whose religious beliefs are incomplete. Despite potential animosity between the two branches of Islam, Sunni–Shia conflicts are not common, mostly because the Sunni populations live in isolated areas along the border of Iran and are not integrated into the national society.

There are other forms of Islam found in Iran as well, including a small but influential population of *Ismailis,* another sect of Shia Islam,

TABLE 1−2

Religious Groups in Iran

Religion	Language Spoken	Population
Shia Moslem	Persian, Azari	58,000,000
Sunni Moslem	Arabic, Baloch, Kurdish	5,200,000
Zoroastrian	Persian	32,000
Armenian Christian	Armani	250,000
Assyrian Christian	Assyrian	35,000
Jewish	Persian, Kurdish	50,000
Baha'i	Persian, Azari	350,000

Source: Estimated from several sources; see Metz, 1987.

and *Sufis*. The Sufis are particularly interesting and have played an important role in Iranian history. Sufism is the mystical or spiritual branch of Islam. Sufis seek to find the true nature of God through meditation, chant, whirling, fasting, or other practices. Even though Sufism is popular among the middle and upper classes in many Islamic societies, it generally rejects material success and favors asceticism. Sufis also believe in individual freedoms and oppose any restraints on human actions, including those imposed by governments. As a result, Sufism has often been unpopular with governmental authorities, especially in authoritarian regimes. The Sufi movement was instrumental in bringing Shia Islam to Iran in the 16th century. However, Sufism is now regarded with suspicion by the present Islamic rulers, who see its spiritual nature and nonauthoritarian attitudes as a threat. There are no estimates of the numbers of Sufis in Iran, since they belong to private and sometimes secret brotherhoods, but several important Sufi brotherhoods have their headquarters in Iran. Their importance, however, is less in their number than in the position of Sufis in prominent governmental and intellectual roles.

Christians

Other religions besides Islam are also found in Iran, some of which have ancient roots. Iran has an indigenous Christian population of Armenians, estimated at 250,000, and Assyrians, perhaps 32,000. Both of these groups have lived in Iran for centuries and, especially the Assyrians, are among the oldest Christian sects in the world. They were in Iran long before the advent of Islam. Both the Armenians and the Assyrians are largely urbanized and found primarily in the northwest section of Iran. Each has its own native language, but both are bilingual in Persian and well-integrated into Persian culture and society.

Christians are generally accepted in Islamic societies. Islam recognizes Christians, as well as Jews, as "People of the Book," meaning that they come from the same religious tradition that began with the prophet Abraham. Moslems do believe, however, that Christian belief is incomplete, since Christians do not believe in Mohammed. Moslems are aware of the roots of Islam in Judaism and Christianity. Islam accepts Jesus as a prophet, although not the son of God, and accepts most of the Old Testament prophets. Christians have historically been given a protected status in Islamic communities, although they usually pay a special tax and have other restrictions placed on them. In Iran, most Christians have accommodated to Iranian life over the centuries and have integrated into many aspects of Iranian society.

The coming of the Islamic revolution in 1979 brought new concerns and worries to the Christian communities in Iran regarding their treatment by the new Islamic government. However, the new constitution of the Islamic Republic, written and ratified in 1979, recognizes both the Armenians and the Assyrians as official religious minorities. These two Christian communities are thus provided constitutional protection from persecution as long as they agree to observe Islamic laws that relate to attire, the prohibition of alcohol, and the segregation of the sexes in public. Although there has been some resentment of these Islamic restrictions among these Christian groups in Iran, especially regarding the segregation of the sexes, they have largely been observed. These traditional Christian groups in modern Iran have survived and largely not been bothered or persecuted, as some of the other non-Islamic groups have.

The new constitution, however, does not recognize other Christian groups as official religious minorities, including small numbers of Roman Catholics, Anglicans, and other Protestant communities. These Christians were converted to Christianity by Western missionaries over the last two hundred years. There were reports of Anglicans being harassed in the period soon after the Islamic Revolution, and some of the leaders of these Christian groups have been jailed by the Islamic government. These forms of Christianity, as distinct from the Assyrian and Armenian churches, are not indigenous to Iran and are associated in the mind of the Iranian Moslems with Western influence and interference. They have thus been suspect and continue to find their situation in Iran precarious.

Jews

Like Christians, Jews are given a protected status in Islam. Almost all Islamic countries have, or had, large Jewish communities. The Jewish community in Iran is one of the oldest in the world, some being the descendants of the Jews of Babylon who were freed by the Iranian Achaemenian dynasty, 550–330 BC. Many Iranian Jews also came to Iran from Iraq in the period after World War II. There were about 85,000 Jews in Iran before the Islamic revolution, many in successful and important positions. The number is thought to be closer to 50,000 at this time.

The Iranian Jews live mostly in the urban areas of Tehran, Isfahan, and Shiraz, although small Jewish communities can usually be found in most Iranian cities. Over the centuries the Jews have assimilated into Iranian culture, and most speak Persian as their native tongue. Although they were once impoverished, they have done particularly well since World War II, especially in the bazaar and in certain professions such as dentistry and pharmacy.

While the Jews, like the Christians, are protected from religious persecution by the 1979 constitution, they are nonetheless under some suspicion in Iran because of their ties to Israel, since Iran is strongly anti-Israel. During the last three decades, over 35,000 Iranian Jews have immigrated to Israel, and as a result many Iranian Jews have family and other connections in Israel. There are large Iranian Jewish immigrant communities in Israel, particularly in the area around Tel Aviv, and it is natural that Iranian Jews would be in touch with relatives in Israel through the mail or phone, or other forms of communication. In 1979, the Iran government charged some Iranian Jews with spying for Israel on the basis of telephone or mail connections to Israel, and some prominent Jews were executed. More recent reports, however, suggest that the Jewish community is surviving, maybe even thriving, and has come to terms with the Islamic government, and it with them.

Zoroastrians

Zoroastrianism is truly an Iranian religion. It developed in Iran in the seventh century BC and became the official religion of the Sassanian Empire in Iran, AD 224–651. Zoroastrianism is a religion that follows the teachings of *Zoroaster* as laid out in the *Avesta*, the holy book of the Zoroastrians. Zoroastrianism was one of the first monotheistic faiths. Zoroastrianism is characterized by a strong belief that life is a struggle between good and evil, and that the responsibility of mankind is to uphold the good. These early concepts of right and wrong are thought to have influenced Judaism, and as a consequence Christianity and Islam. There are still Zoroastrians in Iran, although many were forced to flee or convert to Islam during the Arab conquest in the seventh century. There are now large communities of Zoroastrians in Bombay and other parts of India, where they are called *"Parsis,"* meaning "Persians."

There are about 30,000 Zoroastrians left in Iran, mostly in Tehran and the desert cities of Kerman and Yazd. Zoroastrians were persecuted during some historical periods, but they have largely been accepted by Islam. The constitution of 1979 recognizes Zoroastrianism as an official religious minority, and they are therefore protected from religious persecution. The 1979 constitution also allows them one seat in the Iranian national parliament, the *Majlis.*

Some Zoroastrians were arrested in the period immediately after the Islamic revolution, however, largely because they held high-level positions in the government of Mohammed Reza Shah, the last monarch of Iran. As will be discussed later, Mohammed Reza Shah attached great importance to the pre-Islamic period in Iran, in part to counter the

growing Islamic influence in Iran. As a result, he took a number of steps
to encourage the Zoroastrian community, including offering incentives
for Zoroastrians to move to Iran from India, the preservation of Zoroastrian monuments in Iran, and the promotion of Zoroastrians to important positions in his government. None of these actions pleased the Islamic religious leaders, and when the Shah was overthrown in 1979,
there were some reprisals against the Zoroastrian community. Many
Zoroastrians who could fled to the West.

Baha'is

Bahaism is another religion indigenous to Iran. Bahaism developed in
southern Iran during the 1840s, originally as a reform movement within
Shia Islam. At first it had a large following among the Shia clergy, but
the Islamic leaders soon turned against it as they came to see Bahaism as
a new and threatening religion, and the leader, Baha Allah (1817–1892),
as a false prophet. The hostility among the Islamic clergy toward Bahaism has remained intense. Since Bahaism grew out of Islam, they are
considered **apostates,** that is, people who have abandoned their true
faith. Apostacism is a serious offense in Islam, even punishable by death
in some instances.

In the late nineteenth century the leader of the Baha'i faith was
forced to flee Iran to Ottoman Palestine, now Israel, and there Bahaism
grew into a world religion, teaching equality of the sexes, pacifism, and
tolerance for all religions. Most Baha'is in Iran are Persian speakers and
live in small villages on the southern end of the Iranian Plateau, although
there are many in Tehran and the southern city of Shiraz, where the
movement began. Many Iranian academics and intellectuals are Baha'is.
In the period after the Islamic revolution, Baha'is were attacked by angry
mobs, and more than 700 Baha'i leaders were detained and many killed.
Those who could fled to the West.

CONCLUSION

As this chapter has shown, Iran is a diverse country. It is a country of
high mountains and inhospitable deserts. The Persian language and
culture dominate the country, and the country is overwhelmingly
Moslem, mostly of the Shi'ite branch. Yet, other languages, cultures,
and religions exist in Iran. Diversity naturally creates challenges to national unity, but Iran has generally been able to accommodate these
various diverse elements and maintain a relatively homogenous national identity. However, the challenge will intensify as the pressure
from various groups for increasing independence and cultural auton-
omy intensifies.

In the last decade, the world has seen the decline of imperial nation-
states and the increase in secessionist activities of various ethnolinguistic

and religious groups. In some cases, the results of increasing nationalist sentiments have not been pretty, as old ethnic animosities have led to genocide and ethnic cleansing when ethnic groups have succeeded in gaining power over others. At this time, ethnic tensions are low in Iran, since Iranians continue to focus on the aftermath of the great Islamic revolution of 1979. But the potential for ethnic, religious, and regional conflict remains, and it could tear Iran apart in the future.

CHAPTER 2

The Historical Context

INTRODUCTION: THE HISTORICAL LEGACY

An important part of a country's story is its historical past. History is more than a chronology of past events; it provides the background for an understanding of the shape and texture of a society. The history of a country tells us the story of its beginnings and of its development. By knowing the historical events that the people in the country themselves find important, we are able to see the origins of their values and attitudes, and the events that they feel shaped their lives and their culture. Just as one could not fully understand the United States without knowing the stories of the American Revolution, the Civil War, and the settling of the Western Frontier, one also cannot fully understand Iranian society without knowing the stories of the great pre-Islamic dynasties, the story of the coming of Islam, and the story of the Islamic revolution in 1979.

In some societies, their histories are relatively short. More than half of the countries in the United Nations were created after the Second World War. As sovereign nations their histories are new, although their histories as peoples may go much further back. Other societies have histories that are much older. A few societies are able to trace their history back thousands of years. Iran is one of these societies. Unlike other areas of the Moslem world, Iranians are aware of and proud of their long history, including the period before the advent of Islam in the seventh century AD. In fact, the history of Iran goes back more than 3,500 years.

Finally, the history of Iran is an important part of the Iranian story because its influence can still be found in modern Iranian society. Many of the social characteristics, the values and attitudes, and the social institutions have ancient roots. Iranians know their history. It is important to them, and it is important that Westerners at least have a basic grasp of this.

THE ORIGINS: THE COMING OF THE ARYANS

Evidence of human existence in the area that is now Iran can be traced through skeletal and stone tool remains found in various parts of Iran dating from the Middle Paleolithic, or Stone Age, approximately 50,000 BC (Wilber, 1976:16). Evidence of permanent settled villages engaging in agriculture are found in Iran dating from as far back as 6000 BC (Metz, 1987:5). By 4000 BC an advanced civilization had developed in southwestern Iran; these people are generally called Elamites. The Elamites built the ancient city of Susa and developed a semipictographic writing form that was highly advanced for its time. By 2000 BC the Elamites had become a powerful empire and had conquered the Mesopotamian city of Ur.

Despite these important historical events, the real history of Iranian culture begins with the introduction of Indo-European society into the region in the second millennium BC. The Iranian Plateau was settled in about 1500 BC by Aryan tribes that migrated from the north of Iran and mixed with local peoples. These Aryan tribes were an early branch of the Indo-Europeans. The origins of the Aryan, or Indo-European, culture is not known, but it is thought that it originated in the area of what is now Central Asia, perhaps from the area around Aral Sea, which is in the modern country of Uzbekistan, although some scholars place their origin in Northern Europe (Ghirshman, 1964). Indo-European culture would also eventually spread west across Europe. Some of these Aryan tribes settled in the Central Plateau of what is now southern Iran and became known as the Iranians. Other Aryan tribes eventually settling in the Indian subcontinent. Most modern Iranians have a strong sense of this "Aryan" background.

Scholars attempting to discover what the first Indo-European societies might have been like or what the original Indo-European language might have been look to the ancient Iranian stories and myths, along with those of India, since Iranian culture represents one of the oldest existing ties to this prehistoric Indo-European past. Also, since the Iranians are descendants of the Indo-Europeans, Iranian culture is related, albeit in the distant past, to European culture.

PRE-ISLAMIC IRAN: THE CREATION OF AN IRANIAN SOCIETY 559 BC TO AD 650

Although Islam is now an important part of Iranian society, Iran had a long history before Islam arrived in the seventh century. The first major Iranian empire was the Achaemenian, 559–330 BC. The Achaemenians created the largest empire in the world at that time, spreading Iranian culture from North Africa to the Indian subcontinent. Among the important leaders of this dynasty were Cyrus the Great, who founded the dynasty, and Darius the Great, who captured Egypt and led many battles against the Greeks. The Achaemenians built the great city of Persepolis, the remains of which still exist in the southern Iranian province of Fars.

The Achaemenians were eventually defeated by Alexander the Great in 330 BC, which resulted in the decline of Iranian rule for several centuries, and the control of this area by non-Iranians until the third century AD.

The next great Iranian dynasty was the Sassanian, AD 224–651. The Sassanians reunited the area of greater Iran under Iranian rule and restored much of the glory of the former Achaemenian dynasty. Although the Zoroastrian religion had existed in Iran for many centuries, the Sassanians made it the state religion and Zoroastrian priests played an important role in the society. The Sassanians were able to expand the borders of Iran, and for 200 years fought with the Roman Empire for control over Asia Minor. The Sassanians were finally defeated, as Iran was conquered by the Arabs in AD 641 and Iran again entered a long period of being ruled by non-Iranians.

These pre-Islamic Iranian dynasties were important in shaping the development of modern Iranian society in several ways. For one, in this early period, especially the Sassanian era, a relationship between secular leadership and spiritual leadership emerged that anticipated the modern debate in Iran regarding the role of Islam in government. Zoroastrian priests had a prominent role in the Sassanian government, and the role of government was defined as pursuing the goals set by the religion.

Another characteristic of these early Iranian dynasties that has influenced modern Iran is the system of rigid social hierarchies, including a fixed class system. In the Sassanian period there were three elite classes: the imperial family and large landowning families, the Zoroastrian priesthood, and small landowners (Bill, 1972). This hierarchical system, with some modification, continues to characterize Iranian society today. This rigid system of social classes marks Iranian society as different from other Middle Eastern societies, especially the Semitic societies, which exhibit a more egalitarian social tradition, having descended from nomadic tribes. It may be that the tendency to form hierarchical social systems predates these early Iranian societies and is an ancient Indo-European cultural trait. Many of the societies that have descended from Indo-European roots are highly stratified. These include, in addition to the Iranian class system the Indian caste system and European feudalism.

Finally, this pre-Islamic period is important because it gives Iran a distinctive history from the rest of the Islamic Middle East and is, therefore, important in shaping Iranian nationalism. To this day, Iranians tell and retell the stories and legends of this pre-Islamic period. These stories emphasize the glory of the ancient Iranian past and tell of the heroic deeds of ancient kings and warriors. These legends of the pre-Islamic past are an important part of Iranian popular culture, emphasizing the special and unique qualities of Iranian society. These legends remind the Iranians that they are a special people with a long and glorious history. Although based on historical people or events, most of these stories are mythical. Many are gathered in the *Shah Nameh*, the Book of Kings, which was put into written verse by the famous Iranian poet Ferdowsi in the 10th century, but they existed as an oral tradition much before then. Professional storytellers today tell and retell these legends in villages and teahouses throughout Iran.

THE COMING OF ISLAM: 650 TO 1501

Islam profoundly changed Iran. Islam arose in the Arabian peninsula in the early part of the seventh century AD and quickly spread to surrounding areas, including Iran. Mohammed was born and raised in the Arabian peninsula in the town, now a city, of Mecca near the Red Sea. He began his ministry in AD 610 and quickly gathered a sizable group of converts. His preaching was not thought highly of among the powerful Meccans, and in AD 622 Mohammed was forced to flee to Yathrib, now called Medina, an oasis town about 200 miles northeast of Mecca. The migration of Mohammed and his followers to Medina (this migration is called the *hijra* in Arabic) led to the development of Islam as an important religious and political movement. This date, AD 622, marks the beginning of the Islamic calendar. Mohammed eventually returned triumphantly to Mecca in AD 630 and died in AD 632 (Bates and Rassam, 1983).

Islam quickly became a powerful Arab political and military movement. Beginning during the Prophet Mohammed's life and continuing in the decades after his death, Arab armies spread quickly to other parts of the nearby world, including Iran. Within a short time Arab armies had taken Islam to the borders of China in the east and to Spain in the west. The first Arab conquerors discouraged non-Arabs, including Iranians, from becoming Moslems, since Islam was viewed by the Arabs as a religion only for the Arabs. However, within a short period of time other groups, including Iranians, began to be accepted into Islam (Bates and Rassam, 1983).

The Sassanian Empire fell to the Arabs in AD 641, and gradually the Zoroastrian religion was replaced by Islam. With Islam came Arab culture, and for the next several hundred years in Iran, Arabic was the language of the ruling class, although Persian continued to be spoken by the average person.

As Islam spread, it profoundly changed the societies it conquered, including Iran. By the same token, as other societies joined the Islamic religious community, they brought changes to Islamic philosophy and society. By the eighth century Islam had taken a strong hold in Iran and brought profound changes to Iranian society. However, Persian culture also influenced Islamic culture. Many of the early Islamic scholars, philosophers, and scientists were Iranians (Wickens, 1976). As with most cultural matters, the Iranians accepted Islam but changed it into something uniquely Iranian.

THE RETURN OF IRANIAN RULE: 1501 TO 1850

After several centuries of being ruled by Arabs, Buyids, Seljuk Turks, and Mongols, Iranian rule reemerged in 1501 under the leadership of

Ismail I, who founded what is now called the Safavid dynasty (1501–1722), named after Shaykh Safi ad Din (died circa 1334) to whom Shah Ismail I and his descendants traced their ancestry. The Safavids, although Turkic speakers themselves, established a ruling elite that was eventually referred to as the "guarded domain of Iran," and they therefore are seen by historians as the first native Iranian dynasty to rule Iran after nearly 1,000 years, although they depended heavily on Turkic tribesmen for military support. The Safavids recaptured most of the territory that had been part of earlier Iranian dynasties and returned Iran to much of its former glory. The Safavids adopted Shi'ism as the official religion, although it was not the religion practiced by most of the people in Iran at that time. But by adopting Shi'ism as the state religion, the Safavids were able to carve out a version of Islam that was different from the rest of the Islamic world. Although there are many Shia Moslems in the world who are not Iranian, this version of Islam has over the centuries taken on many characteristics of Iranian culture and temperament.

An important development in Iranian society during this period was the continued evolution of the theocratic state in which government and religion are closely intertwined. Ismail, the first Safavid shah, declared himself both the supreme religious leader and supreme political leader, recognizing that these two forms of leadership were closely interwoven, but separate, functions. The role of religion that developed during this period, and remains the role to this day in Iran, was one in which the religious leaders were to observe, consult, and approve the actions of the government as they deemed those actions consistent with the laws and tenets of Islam, but not to participate in the day-to-day operation of the government. This "advise and consent" role of religion anticipated the role of the Islamic clergy in government as delineated in the constitution of the Islamic Republic written and ratified in 1979.

The most important of the Safavid rulers was Shah Abbas, 1587–1629. He expanded the boundaries of Iran, strengthened the government bureaucracy, moved the capital to Isfahan, built many beautiful buildings and mosques, and was a great patron of the arts, including music and painting. As the previous dynasties had battled against the Greeks and the Romans on the western border, so the Safavids fought with the Ottoman Empire that ruled from Istanbul.

After Shah Abbas, the Safavid dynasty weakened, and in 1722, Isfahan was taken by a small group of Afghan tribesmen who essentially brought the Safavid dynasty to an end. The Afghans were soon driven out in 1736, by Nader Shah, an Afshar tribesman. Nader Shah led military campaigns as far as India, but his rule was brief and he was murdered by his own tribesmen. Several dynasties followed, including the Zand (1750–1794), the Qajar (1795–1925), and the Pahlavi (1925–1979), and while the names and faces changed, the pattern of monarchs and their religious overseers would continue until 1979.

THE COMING OF THE WEST: 1850 TO 1900

Beginning in the early part of the 19th century, Iran began to confront a powerful new force that would have a profound effect on the country. This force was westernization. Actually, however, from its earliest periods, Iran has continuously had relationships with the countries and cultures on its western border, sometimes friendly, but more often hostile. For most of its existence, Iran has looked westward for enlightenment and for territory. In the earliest times, great wars were fought with the Greeks. Yet Greek architecture, art, science, and medicine greatly influenced these early Iranian societies. In the Sassanian period (AD 224–641), Iran battled the Roman and Byzantine cultures on its western border. In the Safavid period (AD 1502–1722), Iran again found itself confronted by pressures from the west as it confronted the Ottoman Empire in Istanbul. The Safavids and the Ottomans were at times great enemies, but their cultures strongly influenced each other as well. Many Iranian customs and institutions derive from the Ottomans.

These historical conflicts with societies to its west did not prepare Iran for the challenges brought by the onslaught of European culture beginning in the early part of the 19th century. For almost two centuries Iran would find itself being pushed back and forth between European powers, mostly the British and the Russians, and later the Americans.

Western interests in Iran were, and are, largely strategic. European powers were interested in Iran largely because of its important location, and because of the profits to be made by exploiting its resources. Europe had little intrinsic interest in Iranian culture or society. In the early 19th century, Britain became concerned with protecting trade routes to its colonies in Asia, particularly India, and the Russian Empire was interested in expanding its southern border. By 1850, Iran had fought two losing wars with the Russian Empire in the Caucasus, and in the 1860s Iran lost its holding in Central Asia to Russian expansion. At the southern border, the British landed troops in Iran several times during the middle part of the 19th century, mostly to pressure Iran into staying out of Afghanistan, where the British had interests (Metz, 1987).

Western influence changed Iranian political values as well, and led Iranians to attempt to emulate European models of government and education. A few Iranians began visiting and studying in Europe in the middle of the 19th century. They were impressed with European technology and culture. These returning Iranians brought Western ideas back to Iran, and pressure began to grow in Iran to reform the governmental structure, which to that time had been monarchical without constitutional constraint. The movement to create a constitutional monarchy, as found in Europe, began to grow. In 1871, Naser ed-Din Shah, the ruling monarch of Iran at that time, established a European-style cabinet with administrative responsibilities, although he stopped short of creating a constitution (Metz, 1987). The pressure to reform the government along European lines would continue.

Beyond the military and political pressures on Iranian society, the major, and most obviously self-serving, intrusion of the Western powers into Iran, and eventually the most offensive to the Iranian people, was the economic exploitation of Iran. The exploitation of Iranian resources was largely accomplished through concessions given to Western countries and individuals that were in essence monopolies over large segments of the Iranian economy. For instance, in the second half of the 19th century, all railroad construction and all banking were conceded to the British. In 1880 a British company was given a monopoly over Iran's tobacco trade. Other concessions to foreign companies or governments would follow (Metz, 1987).

While the economic concessions were granted by the ruling monarchs, the average Iranian found them offensive and opposition began to grow. The tobacco concession particularly hit a nerve, creating an angry backlash in the streets of Iran. The Islamic clergy took a stand against this foreign intervention, and in 1890 issued a *fatwa*, a religious ruling, banning tobacco use, essentially halting tobacco trade in Iran. This public revolt, now called the **tobacco rebellion,** forced the shah to withdraw the tobacco concession and set the stage for a battle over foreign concessions that would go on for much of the 20th century (Keddie, 1981).

THE CONSTITUTIONAL REVOLUTION: 1900 TO 1921

This tobacco rebellion did not end the concessions that gave Iranian resources to foreign companies, and the hostility among the Iranian people to them continued to grow. By the beginning of the 20th century the battle lines for the control of Iran were set. On one side were the Qajar rulers, whose dynasty was coming to an end after nearly 200 years. They would later be replaced by the Pahlavi dynasty, but the beginning of the end for ruling monarchies had begun. By the beginning of the 20th century the power of the Qajars had considerably weakened. They had become corrupt, oppressive, and increasingly irrelevant. As a consequence the Qajar royal family had become unpopular with the average Iranians, who saw their standard of life deteriorating while the shah and his people continued a lavish lifestyle. To the Qajar shahs and princes, of which there were many, Europe appeared to be a solution to their problems. They were attracted to the modern lifestyles of the Europeans and envied the lives of European royalty. And they badly needed the foreign money gained by giving foreign concessions to keep their monarchy and opulent lifestyle afloat.

On the other hand, the dawning of the 20th century saw a growing backlash to the foreign influence in Iran. This backlash was led by a number of interested parties. The Islamic clergy were against the concessions to Western countries, in part because they feared the secular influence of the West on Iran, and also because they wanted a greater voice for Islam in the Iranian government. The Western intervention in Iran was also opposed by secular nationalists. These were Iranian intellectuals, many of whom had been educated in the West. These secular nationalists were sympathetic to Western ideas, especially those dealing with democracy and representative government, but were against the economic exploitation of Iranian resources. Their goals were quite different from those of the Islamic clergy, with whom they often cooperated in opposition to the ruling monarchy. Their numbers were small at the beginning of the 20th century, but, along with the religious leaders, they would play an increasingly important role in Iranian society as the century unfolded.

Finally, foreign concessions and the growing power of foreign companies and governments were opposed by the Iranian merchants and artisans who formed the backbone of the country's economy. Referred to collectively as the *bazaar,* since most businesses are located in the central bazaars of the major cities, these traditional businessmen were, and still are, an important social, economic, and political force in Iran. They are traditionally conservative and tend to side with the religious clergy on political issues. The bazaar controls the purse strings in Iran and can, and periodically does, exercise its power by closing, essentially halting all business in Iran. These traditional Iranian businessmen do not oppose foreign investment or international trade, but they reject the control of this trade by foreign companies.

As the 20th century unfolded, the pressure from Britain and Russia for military and economic concessions continued to increase. The Qajar finances were in bad shape, and the Iranian treasury depended heavily on money from these concessions to foreign companies and from loans made by the British and the Russian governments. The Russians especially had loaned a considerable amount of money to the Qajars and became increasingly concerned about Iran's ability to repay the loans. The Qajar shah at that time, Muzaffar ad Din (1896–1907), had used much of the money from these loans to finance trips to Europe and for his own extravagance. As collateral for these loans, Russia demanded and received the rights to all of Iran's customs income, except those from Gulf ports. Russia also established a "sphere of influence" in northern Iran, and Britain in southern Iran, where they were given the right to operate without the interference of the Iranian government. To make matters worse, in 1901 the Qajar government granted the British a 60-year concession to exploit Iran's oil resources.

The movement in Iran intensified to curb the influence of foreign companies and to bring the royal government under control. Voices in Iran begin to demand a more representative government with a consultative assembly along the lines of a European-style parliament. In 1906, 10,000 people, led by bazaar merchants, occupied the British legation to protest the monarchy's failure to change. The Qajar monarch, Shah Muzaffar ad Din, was forced to convene a national assembly to draw up a constitution. The constitution created by this assembly defined sharp limitations on the power of the monarchy, created an elected parliament, or *majlis* in Persian, and a cabinet subject to confirmation by the *majlis.*

Although bitterly opposed to the constitution, the shah signed the new constitution on December 30, 1906. He died five days later. Iran had entered the 20th century, both figuratively and literally. The **Constitutional Revolution,** as this event is now called, marks the beginning of the modern period in Iran.

Despite the apparent victory over the Qajar monarchy and its foreign supporters, the new constitution was never really implemented. The next Qajar monarch, Mohammed Ali Shah, was determined to crush the new constitution. After a series of clashes with the new *majlis,* Mohammed Ali Shah bombed the *majlis* building in June of 1908 with the help of the Russian-trained and -led Cossack Brigade—while the *majlis* was in session! He arrested many of the deputies and dismissed the *majlis.* Mohammed Ali Shah was temporarily forced to flee to Russia from pressure by the constitutional forces in 1909, but he returned to reclaim his throne in 1910 with the support of Russian-led troops.

Not only did the constitutional movement falter because of the opposition of the Qajar rulers, but European influence continued to increase unabated after 1906 as well. In 1907 the British and the Russians signed the Anglo-Russian Agreement, in which they agreed to further split Iran into two spheres of influence. The Russians were given almost complete control over the northern areas of Iran to pursue their economic and military interests. The British were given exclusive rights to the southern areas of Iran. In 1911 the *majlis* tried to reassert its rights by hiring the American businessman William Morgan Shuster to reorganize the government's finances, aiming largely to control the corrupt and lavish expenses of the royalty. When Shuster directed the tax authorities to collect taxes from the upper class, they appealed to Russia, who threatened to occupy Tehran, forcing Shuster to resign.

REZA SHAH PAHLAVI: 1921 TO 1941

By 1914, at the onset of World War I, Iran was in a precarious position. The Qajar dynasty that had ruled since 1795 was essentially dead, although a Qajar shah would rule until 1925, albeit in name only. The constitutional movement had written a constitution that had created a European-style constitutional monarchy, but it had never really been implemented. And Western meddling was growing stronger—Russia controlling the north and Britain the south. During World War I Iran tried to stay out of the conflict by declaring itself neutral. Given Iran's location near Turkey and with British and Russian troops stationed in Iran, this proved to be impossible. Britain grew concerned about German sympathies among some Iranian leaders and increased its presence in Iran by creating a British-led Iranian military unit called South Persia Rifles to protect its interests in southern Iran. Thus, by the end of World War I the presence of Britain had increased, but Russia, in contrast, was preoccupied with its own revolution, and interest in Iran momentarily waned (Metz, 1987).

In 1919, Britain overplayed its hand. Britain tried to forced the shah of Iran to sign an agreement, referred to as the Anglo-Persian Agreement, in which Britain would provide Iran with loans and, in turn, take over most of Iran's affairs, in effect making Iran a British protectorate. This agreement was widely unpopular in Iran and the *majlis* refused to ratify it. Although Ahmad Shah actually refused to sign the agreement, it was signed by his prime minister; this event was nonetheless the last straw for the Qajar monarchy. In 1921 the Russian Cossack Brigade, which was manned by Iranian soldiers trained by Russians and led by an Iranian named Reza Khan, marched into Tehran and seized power (Metz, 1987).

Reza Khan quickly moved to take over Iran and formed a new government, first naming himself minister of war, and then in 1923, prime minister. Although he briefly considered making Iran a republic, he named himself shah in 1926, replacing Ahmad Shah, the last of the Qajar shahs, who had actually fled Iran several years earlier. Reza Khan selected for his dynastic name Pahlavi, which refers to middle Persian, the official language of the pre-Islamic Sassanian dynasty and the language of the Zoroastrian religion.

Reza Khan, now Reza Shah, began an aggressive program to modernize Iran. Like Mustafa Kemal Ataturk, who ruled Turkey at that time, and other leaders across the Middle East, Reza Shah sought to modernize Iran by the wholesale adoption of Western methods, ideas, and technology. With the assistance of Western-trained Iranians, mostly from the military, he modernized the military, overhauled the government bureaucracy, and pressed for modern economic expansion. Like Ataturk, he saw the Islamic clergy as a major obstacle to modernization and moved quickly to secularize the schools, to ban religious dress, and to create secular courts. He outlawed the use of the veil for women, and in 1936 Reza Shah's wife and daughters appeared in public without their veils, the first time this had happened in Iranian history (Metz, 1987). When the religious leaders protested, he was quick to use force, and many religious leaders were arrested and killed.

While Reza Shah borrowed much from the West, he also moved aggressively against Western political and economic influence in Iran. He abolished most concessions to foreign businesses and in 1928 withdrew the right of Westerners living in Iran not to be tried in Iranian courts. In 1932 Reza Shah canceled the agreement under which the Anglo-British Oil Company, the predecessor to British Petroleum, produced and exported Iranian oil. The British eventually forced Reza Shah to sign a new agreement, again giving Britain the rights to Iran's oil, but bad feelings between Britain and Iran had been created.

Reza Shah was a forceful and ruthless leader. His aggressive programs to modernize Iran accomplished a great deal. He built roads, established a modern university, and built a modern economy that brought prosperity to many. More importantly, he brought stability to a country that had drifted chaotically for many decades under corrupt and inept rulers. Consequently many Iranians were tolerant of his heavy-handed methods in the beginning. Over time, however, his repressive measures increased and the Iranian people began to turn against him. He took power away from the *majlis*, muzzled the press, and arrested many of his enemies. His harshest attacks were on the Islamic clergy. In 1936 he lost all support from the religious elements in Iran when his troops took the unprecedented step of firing on religious worshippers who had gathered at the holy shrine of Imam Reza in Mashad (Metz, 1987). His policy of canceling foreign concessions lost him any support he had from foreign governments. On the eve of World War II, Reza Shah had managed to antagonize both the British and the Russians, and had lost most of the support he had among the Iranian people.

MOHAMMED REZA SHAH PAHLAVI: 1941 TO 1979

As World War II began, Reza Shah sought to stay out of the war by declaring Iran's neutrality, as Iran had tried to do in World War I. The allies, particularly Britain, did not trust Reza Shah. When British–Iranian relations soured in the 1930s, Reza Shah had moved his foreign policy in the direction of Germany. As World War II approached, Germany had become Iran's largest trading partner, and many German nationals lived in Iran as advisors and businessmen. The Allies were also concerned that Reza Shah had attempted to curry favors from Germany by playing up Iran's Aryan heritage. In 1935 Reza Shah asked the international community to change the name of the country from Persia, the old Greek name, to Iran so as to emphasize the Aryan connection and to appeal to German sentiments (Yarshater, 1997).

When Germany invaded the Soviet Union in 1941, the Allies needed a route to send supplies to the Soviet front, and travel across Iran was the obvious choice. However, to use Iranian soil for the war effort would be to violate its neutrality. Reza Shah was forced to abdicate when the Soviet Union and Britain put military pressure on Iran. Reza Shah was escorted by the British first to Mauritius and then to South Africa, where he died in 1944. Reza Shah's young son, Mohammed Reza Shah, assumed the throne and quickly signed a treaty with the British and the Russians, allowing war materials to travel overland to the Soviet front. In turn the two allies agreed to respect Iranian independence. In 1943, Iran joined the war by declaring war on Germany, thus qualifying for membership in the United Nations.

Mohammed Reza Shah's reign would last for 38 years. It would be one of the longest in Iranian history and one of the most turbulent. When he was finally swept out of power by the forces of the Islamic revolution in 1979, he would be the last of the great Iranian shahs, ending a history of monarchs going back to the Safavid dynasty of the 16th century, and even to the pre-Islamic monarchies before that. Mohammed Reza Shah's reign would take Iran from the turmoil of World War II through a period of nationalism and economic development, and finally to the emergence of the militant Islamic state. Mohammed Reza Shah's ambition, like his father's, was to build a modern country on the model of the West, particularly the United States. Because of its oil resources, Iran would become a world power under Mohammed Reza Shah's leadership, amassing a large modern army. A large professional middle class would grow and the country would develop an industrial base and a prosperous middle class. Thousands of Iranians would travel overseas each year, particularly to the United States, to study, and thousands of foreigners, many of them Americans, would live in Iran as advisors, teachers, and businessmen during these 38 years. Tehran would become a modern city, with modern buildings, restaurants, and shops. Mohammed Reza Shah would build modern universities in all of the major cities in Iran, including Pahlavi University in the city of Shiraz, which was built on the model of an American university with classes in English and named after his dynasty.

During his reign, Mohammed Reza Shah faced two great political crises, one which he overcame, with foreign help, and one which he did not. The first great challenge came early in his reign, and arose from the secular nationalist movement that objected to Mohammed Reza Shah's orientation toward the British, and particularly the oil concessions enjoyed by the Anglo-Iranian Oil Company. These concessions were not of Mohammed Reza Shah's doing, or for that matter the doing of his father, who in fact had tried to undo them. Nonetheless, public pressure to end these concessions began to build again in the late 1940s and early 1950s. In 1951, the Iranian *majlis,* under the leadership of a popular Iranian nationalist named Mossadeq, passed a bill nationalizing the oil industry, thus ending any foreign monopolies. This effort led to a major rift with Britain, which was able to bring the Iranian economy to a standstill. Large demonstrations took place against Mohammed Reza Shah, who was seen as pro-British and against the nationalization of the oil industry. As a result, he was forced to flee Iran in August of 1953, and the popular Mossadeq became the temporary leader of the country. The nationalization of the oil industry was seen as a major threat to Western interests, and the United States and Great Britain, led by the CIA, organized a coup d'état against the nationalist government. Pro-shah demonstrations were organized, and after a few days of rioting, with the help of the United States and Britain, the royalist forces were able to regain the upper hand and the shah was able to return (Roosevelt, 1979).

After returning, Mohammed Reza Shah moved against the nationalist forces and many were jailed and killed. (Mossadeq was initially sentenced to three years' imprisonment, but he was allowed to remain under house arrest in his village outside of Tehran until he died in 1967.) Mohammed Reza Shah began an aggressive campaign to modernize and westernize Iran. He introduced a number of reforms in the 1960s that he called the White Revolution. These included agrarian land reform, profit sharing by the industrial workers, the nationalization of forests and pasturelands, changes in the electoral laws to encourage greater participation of workers, and the establishment of a Literary Corps to allow young men to satisfy their military service by teaching basic literacy in rural villages. Later he included voting rights for women.

The reforms of the White Revolution enjoyed considerable support from the Iranian people in the beginning. And in general the economic conditions of Iran improved dramatically in the 1960s and early 1970s, especially in Tehran and other major cities. A large urban middle class of successful businessmen and professionals grew, and many people were better off. However, although the reforms of the White Revolution seemed progressive, they in fact did little to raise the living standards of the average Iranians, particularly the peasant farmers who made up a majority of the Iranian population, and popular unrest began to grow.

The reforms of the White Revolution were particularly opposed by the Islamic clergy. For one, Mohammed Reza Shah's reforms were clearly aimed at building a secular Iran, including such things as rights for women, to which the Shia clergy naturally objected. The Islamic leaders also objected to the agrarian land reform provisions of the White Revolution. Over the centuries large tracts of land had been endowed to Islamic organizations as a part of the traditional Islamic practice of tithing. In essence, Islam had become one of the largest landlords in Iran and the Shah's land reforms threatened their holdings. In 1963, a religious leader named Ayatollah Sayyid Ruhollah Musavi Khomeini gave a fiery speech against the Shah and his reforms in the holy city of Qom. He was arrested and later exiled to Turkey and then to Iraq, where he continued to speak against Mohammed Reza Shah and his secular reforms.

Iranians also began to object to Mohammed Reza Shah's personal lifestyle and his attempts to glorify his personal image. Concerned with producing an heir to the throne, he divorced his first wife in 1948 because she had not produced a son; he divorced his second wife in 1959 for the same reason. He married for a third time in 1959 and the new queen gave birth to a son in 1960. In 1967, he held a grand coronation ceremony for himself (he had actually never been official crowned). He gave himself the title of *Arya-Mehr*, or light of the Aryans, in clear reference to the pre-Islamic dynasties.

Many Moslems in Iran objected to his focus on pre-Islamic Iranian culture and history, and some felt his motive in this was to discredit Islam. In 1971, he held a large celebration to commemorate the anniversary of the founding of Iran by Cyrus the Great, the founder of the Achaemenian dynasty 2,500 years earlier. This celebration angered the Shia clergy, and Ayatollah Khomeini, now in exile in Iraq, spoke out against the celebration. In 1975, the Iranian *majlis*, at Mohammed Reza Shah's request, abandoned the Islamic calendar, which begins with the pilgrimage of Mohammed to Medina in AD 622, and adopted a calendar that begins with the founding of the Achaemenian dynasty by Cyrus the Great in 546 BC. With the stroke of a pen, the calendar year in Iran jumped from 1355 to 2500. Islamic leaders found this outrageous and sacrilegious. To devout Moslems, Mohammed Reza Shah's glorification of Iran's pre-Islamic past was an insult to Islam and to them personally.

THE ISLAMIC REVOLUTION: 1979 AND AFTER

By the middle of the 1970s the rule of Mohammed Reza Shah was becoming problematic, although few predicted that a revolution was brewing. His economic and social reforms had had some success and Iran had made great strides in education, health, and industrialization. Yet he was never able to gain the popularity achieved by his father, and by the mid 1970s opposition to his rule had grown in many parts of Iranian society. His self-aggrandizement offended many Iranians, and his attempts to modernize the country, including the White Revolution, were never very successful because of massive corruption at the highest level. To many Iranians, it seemed that their lot had not improved, while a newly created economic and social elite that surrounded Mohammed Reza Shah and his confidants lived in great luxury.

The modernization of Iran under Mohammed Reza Shah had also brought a massive infusion of Western culture to Iran. By the mid-1970s there were over 60,000 foreigners working and living in Iran, 45,000 of them Americans. American women walked openly on the streets of Iranian cities in shorts and halter tops. Westerners drank alcohol and put on parties at which men and women were present. To many Iranians, American culture with its values of individualism, sexual freedom, and secularism was a threat to traditional Iranian values that stressed obligations to community, family, and religion.

As opposition to the Shah and his government grew, he reacted by becoming increasingly autocratic and harsh. Opposition political parties were essentially banned; opponents were arrested and jailed. Mohammed Reza Shah created a powerful secret police force called SAVAK, an acronym for *Sazman-e Etelaat va Amniyat-e Keshvar*. SAVAK became infamous for domestic surveillance at all levels of Iranian life, as well as for imprisoning and torturing many innocent people.*

In addition to the above problems, Mohammed Reza Shah's rule was finally done in by the severe economic downturn in Iran caused in part by a worldwide inflation and recession beginning in 1975. This led to a dramatic decrease in oil revenues and a period of economic contraction in Iran accompanied with high inflation. The bazaar, which had

---

*Author's Note: In 1973 through 1975 I was a visiting professor at Pahlavi University in the city of Shiraz in southern Iran. I came to know that my lectures were regularly monitored for subversive content by SAVAK agents, who were probably student informants. I was never in danger personally, since if my lectures were found to be somehow offensive to the government I would simply be asked to leave Iran. However, students in my classes could be in trouble with the SAVAK simply for being at my lectures. Over the years that I taught in Iran, many of my students disappeared from sight for a period of a few weeks to six months. No one would comment on their whereabouts, but it was known that they had been arrested by SAVAK. Most would eventually return to class, pale and shaken, and not a word would be said about their absence. Some never returned. Needless to say, this put a chill on class discussions.

largely been behind the shah as long as the economy was doing well, now turned against him.

With the three important forces in Iranian society—the clergy, the secular nationalist, and the bazaar—now united against the shah, antigovernment riots in many Iranian cities began in earnest in 1977 and continued into 1978. The antigovernment demonstrations were led in part by the Islamic leaders. Ayatollah Khomeini was still in exile but began to take an important role in building the revolution. However, the demonstrators included Iranians from all walks of life and all political orientations. The size and energy of the demonstrations, and the anger toward Mohammed Reza Shah, his government, and those who had supported him, surprised many who thought that the shah would be able to maintain his rule indefinitely. The anger suppressed by 38 years of tyranny and oppression had suddenly been unleashed. By autumn of 1978 the country was in full-blown revolt, and in January 1979 the shah fled Iran, never to return. The Pahlavi dynasty was over, and the 2,500-year reign, interrupted intermittently by invaders, had apparently come to an end.

Khomeini returned triumphantly to Tehran on February 1, 1979, as the absolute ruler of Iran. The religious leaders, along with the other segments of Iranian society that had participated in the revolution, began the task of putting Iran back together and sorting out what a new Iran would look like. The first task was to create a new government based on the principles of Islam. A new constitution was drafted to create an Islamic government. It was passed overwhelmingly by a national referendum in December 1979.

Although there had been a great deal of discussion about what an Islamic government might look like—Khomeini himself had written about the role of the clergy in government while in exile—the details of how such a government would actually function had to be worked out. The new Islamic constitution was based to some degree on the French model of government. (Khomeini had been in exile in France just before returning to Iran.) The new Islamic constitution adopted in 1979 called for a parliament and a prime minister, and a strong president separately elected, as in France. To assure that the government adheres to Islamic principles, the new constitution created a position called the *faqih,* a just and pious Islamic jurist, who would have supreme authority over the nation. Khomeini was named the first *faqih* for life, and the process for selecting his successor was described in the new constitution. In addition, a Council of Guardians, to be composed of Islamic clergy, was established by the new constitution to oversee and approve or veto all new laws to make sure that they were correct according to the tenets of Islam.

IRAN NOW

Nearly 20 years have passed since the Islamic revolution. While much of the rhetoric of the revolutionary movement continues, it is also true that, like all revolutionary movements, the hard line taken in the earlier period has softened. A number of themes that emerged during the revolution are still present in Iran and characterize modern Iranian society. For one, the role of the clergy and the role of Islam in Iranian society have been firmly established. Iran has been Islamic since the seventh century, and Islam has always been an important part of life, but since the revolution the role of Islam has increased in almost all areas of society. The role of Islam in Iranian society will be discussed at greater length in Chapter 4.

Iranian society continues to reject much of the culture of the Western world, particularly those parts of Western culture that it finds offensive to Islamic values. Hostility toward the United States remains particularly strong. The United States and Iran still do not have diplomatic relations after almost two decades. In Iran, the United States is still referred to as the Great Satan. (Iran refers to the former Soviet Union as the "Little Satan.") While the stridency has decreased, the anti-US rhetoric has continued.

Iran now is returning to more normal participation in the world of nations. Yet it faces a number of significant problems, including rapid population growth, urban crowding, and a growing rift between traditional and modern elements of society. Many of the best and brightest Iranians have fled to the West over the last two decades. But Iran is attempting to deal with these problems as it tries to create a new society based on Islamic principles. These issues will be taken up in the remainder of this book.

CHAPTER 3

Family, Marriage, and Kinship

INTRODUCTION: FAMILY AND KINSHIP IN IRANIAN SOCIETY

One part of the story of a society is the nature of the social relationships among people based on kinship and marriage. This part of the Iranian story will focus on how family life is structured, how people meet and marry, and how they relate to their more distant relatives. This part of the Iranian story will also look at how the Iranian society defines appropriate roles for women and men, and the opportunities and duties that men and women have in the family and in the society at large.

In Iran, and in the Middle East in general, family life and kinship ties form an important social institution, although changes are also taking place. For Iranians, the obligations, responsibilities, and privileges of kinship are more important than any other kind of social arrangement. The family to whom one belongs (one's father, brothers, and cousins), and in general to whom one is related, determines the kind of political, economic, and social opportunities one will have in life. The family to whom one belongs will determine whom a person marries, where one goes to school, the type of career one has, and, in general, the status of a person in Iranian society. Individuals without close family ties have little status in the Iranian society.

Since the family plays such an important strategic role in one's life, the maintenance of family status and honor is of utmost importance. To ensure that family prestige is maintained in a changing society, family members attempt to position themselves in the social structure to ensure that the family's status is upheld. One son may enter the clergy, for instance, another son the military, and yet another might become an engineer, each prepared to support the other and to protect the family's position as the political and economic climates change.

Iranians also define kinship to its outermost boundary, so that even a distant relative may provide an important connection. In Iran, it is expected that relatives will help one another to find jobs, loan each other money, or in general provide each other with support. Nepotism, which is generally looked down upon in the United States, is common in Iran, and not considered undesirable. After all, who better to ask for help than a relative? Thus, families play a role in social mobility. Successful family members are expected to help more needy relatives. It is the success of the whole family that is important, not the success of a single individual, and thus families rise or fall in the social stratification system together.

Families also play an important role in **social control** of individual behavior. The focus on the importance of family status and honor restrains family members from violating social norms that might embarrass or dishonor the family name. In traditional Iranian society, the family is held directly responsible for the behavior of its members, especially in the violation of moral or religious norms. Until recent times, people caught committing a crime such as adultery or rape were returned to their families to be punished.

THE TRADITIONAL IRANIAN FAMILY

While there is tremendous variation in the structure of the Iranian family, traditional Iranian families are almost always **patriarchal** (authority in the hands of men), **patrilineal** (inheritance through the male line), and **patrilocal** (the bride moves into the husband's place of residence on marriage). The man of the house, usually the father or husband, is the leader of the family and expects obedience and respect from the other members. He in turn is expected to protect and support the family and is responsible for its social, economic, and spiritual needs. Iranian fathers tend to be strict disciplinarians, especially with older sons approaching manhood, although they are often affectionate and loving with the younger children, especially boys. The traditional Iranian husband is the boss, although he is expected to treat his wife with respect and kindness.

Both sons and daughters live at home until they marry. Traditionally single men seldom live away from home, even in their twenties, and unmarried women would never live alone. This is changing for young men, however, as Iran modernizes and men go off to college, or to other cities to find work. Having grown children in the household often leads to conflict in Iranian homes, usually between grown sons and their traditional fathers. This became an issue during the revolution, when the younger generation, imbued with revolutionary fervor, often clashed with the older generation within the household.

The patriarchal structure of the Iranian family does not mean that women do not play an important role, both in the family and in society. Although women have no formal power in the home, Iranian women have important economic and social roles in the family. Women can also play an important role outside the home, and there have been prominent women in Iranian history, although they have always been the wife, daughter, sister, or mother of an important man. A woman's role in Iranian society is always restricted to those arenas considered appropriate for female participation, and a woman's position in society is defined by her relationship to a male relative, usually as a wife or daughter.

Within the family, Iranian women often play a strong role in running the household, raising the children, and making domestic decisions. Most people familiar with Iranian society know that Iranian women are anything but shy and diffident. Since Iranian fathers often spoil the younger children, the mother must also swing the heavy hand of discipline. Mothers usually play an important role in their sons' lives. Like Iranian men, Iranian women, in their own environment, tend to be outgoing and confident, and when given a chance, successful.

Because Iranian families are **patrilineal,** the husband's or father's relatives are given preference over the mother's or the wife's side of the family. Americans tend to be **bilineal** (descent traced in both the male and female side) in that we generally put equal importance on both the mother's and the father's sides of the family, although American women usually, but not always, take their husbands' surname at marriage. Patrilineal descent, however, means more than just how the family name is passed on. It also involves important rights, responsibilities, and duties associated with relatives on the male's side of the family. In Iranian rural society, such things as water rights, land usage, and mutual defense are traditional patrilineal obligations. That is, families connected through the male line, especially brothers and male cousins, are obliged to cooperate and provide each other economic, political, and social support. In urban society, individuals depend on their patrilineal kin for economic help, protection, and general support.

Inheritance also takes place through the male line in Iranian society, both in terms of wealth and political authority. Sons inherit the family status and wealth from their fathers, although in traditional Islamic law daughters are entitled to inheritance, their share being equal to one-half of what a son receives.

The patrilineal system is also used to create communal groupings. Communities of people who are all related along the male line are common in Iran and the Middle East. These groups are called extended families, clans, or, if they are large, tribes. The **patronymic groups,** as anthropologists call them, are the most common form of communal organization in traditional Iranian society and form the basis for much of Iranian social and economic life. In rural Iran, most villages are made up of large extended families, as are many traditional neighborhoods in Iranian cities.

Patrilineal descent is particularly important for some Iranians whose position in society depends on their ability to trace their patrilineal ancestry back many generations, even centuries. Among the Iranian pastoral nomads, for instance, tribal membership is defined by patrilineal descent; all of the members of the tribe are male descendants of the same male ancestor, real or imagined. Since tribal position is based on how closely one is related to this ancestor, tribal genealogies are important and often memorized.

Likewise, knowing one's patrilineal descent is important for those who claim special religious status as descendants of important Islamic saints. The most important of these statuses are those based on being direct patrilineal descendants of the Prophet Mohammed through his daughter Fatima and son-in-law Ali. In Iran these people are called *sayyids,* and in traditional Iranian society they are thought to have spiritual powers to grant special wishes because of their patrilineal connection to the Prophet Mohammed. *Sayyids* are often able to name all of their ancestors back to Mohammed, over 1,400 years ago. The term *sayyid* is used in Iran and other Shia communities as a title of respect indicating spiritual importance. For instance, Ayatollah Khomeini was a *sayyid.*

HOUSEHOLDS, COMPOUNDS, AND EXTENDED FAMILIES

In Iran, there is a difference between a **household** and a **family,** although this distinction may be difficult to make in practice. A family represents a social contract based on blood relation or marriage, that is, a group of people living together as a unit. A household is the economic and residential unit. To most people in the Middle East, including Iranians, the ideal household structure is the patrilineal extended family made up of the father, his wife, the married sons and their families, and all of the unmarried sons and daughters of the father. This ideal household type is not always realized because of the lack of space, family deaths, lack of children, and/or the movement of males to urban areas. In the modern cities extended family households are becoming less common because of space limitations forcing families to live in small apartments.

Traditionally, Iranian extended families live in a compound. A compound is a walled area with rooms arranged around the courtyard and shut off from the outside by a heavy wooden door. Compounds have both communal areas and private areas. Within a compound, each **nuclear family** (that is, each husband, wife, and their children) usually has its own space, which would include a cooking area and sleeping quarters. Other areas would be communal and shared with other nuclear families. For instance, in each compound there is usually a common latrine and sometimes an oven for baking bread that is shared by all of the families in the compound.

Compounds are an ideal living arrangement for extended families. The extended family can live together, yet each nuclear family unit can still have its own privacy. In addition, many family roles and chores can be shared. Those in the family who work outside of the home, mostly the men, usually pool their incomes, or at least all contribute financially to the extended family. In the enclosed compound women share household duties such as child rearing, food preparation, clothes washing, and other domestic tasks. Each generation contributes; young girls watch after the babies, while the older women do other household tasks. Compounds often include members of several generations, and older members of the extended family play important roles. Grandparents are expected to play an important role in the education and socialization of the younger children. In turn, as the elderly become frail, they are cared for in the family compound by members of the younger generations. In traditional Iranian society, there is no need for nursing or rest homes for the elderly. The extended families take care of their own.

This is not to say that the Iranian family compound is an idyllic place. With many people and several generations living close together, tensions arise. Adult children living at home fight with their parents (this is not unique to Iran). In the rapidly changing Iran, the older generation may remember and value the period of Iranian culture common before the Islamic revolution in 1979 during which religion played less of a role in Iranian society, while the younger generation, raised in the highly charged post-revolutionary period, may have different values and commitments. These generational, or cohort, differences often lead to tense compound relations between the generations. "Revolutionary" sons have been known to turn their "reactionary" fathers into the authorities in extreme situations.

Other tensions exist in the compound. Since sons bring their brides into the compound, mothers-in-law are often cruel to their daughters-in-law. Favoritism among the children is common. Boy children play while girls from the earliest ages are made to do chores. In the traditional Iranian family, the favored child is often the youngest son, who is allowed to sit beside his father when receiving guests or at other important ceremonies. Jealousies within the sibling order are intense, especially among the sons, since there is no rule of **primogeniture** (family inheritance going to the oldest son), and intense rivalries between male siblings for parental favor are common. As in all societies, family bickering, backbiting, and gossiping are common within the extended family compound. Within the compound, punishment of childhood misdeeds is usually swift and often harsh. The switch is the favorite instrument for whacking children, and usually is administered by the women.

The extended family compound is found in the Iranian villages and in the traditional parts of most Iranian cities. It is a way of life that has endured in Iran, even in modern times, in large part because it works well in Iranian society. It is an excellent fit of form with function. But this way of life is declining in Iran. Rapid urbanization is breaking up the traditional family, as the young people, mostly the men, are moving to Tehran, or other large Iranian cities, to find work, leaving families all over Iran without productive males in the home. This unprecedented urbanization is also leading to the crowding of the large Iranian cities, mostly Tehran. Compounds take up too much space, and many in the middle class now live in apartments, making extended family living more difficult. The poor moving into the cities cannot even find a comfortable place to live, let alone find a compound for their extended family.

MARRIAGE

Marriage is an important institution in any society. In the Middle East, Islam encourages people to marry, and in Iran marriage regulations are governed by Islamic law. In a society in which kinship relations are important and in which family status and honor must be upheld, marriage is one of the key strategies by which families attempt to improve, or at least maintain, their social position. In traditional Iranian society in rural villages or in nomadic society, the institution of marriage is used to forge strategic linkages with other groups for economic or political gain, such as the sharing of pasturelands or the settlement of old disputes. In modern urban society, particularly among the middle and upper classes, the institution of marriage provides a strategy to move up in the social hierarchy by marrying sons or daughters into other, hopefully, higher-status families. In addition, there is a strong preference for marrying within extended families so as to preserve existing family status.

As a result, the selection of a marriage partner for a son or a daughter is an important family matter, and one for the family elders to decide. Marriages are therefore arranged, usually by the elders in the family, often the women. When a young man is judged ready for marriage, his parents visit the parents of a young women whom they believe will make a good match. The future bride and groom may or may not have met, and may or may not have a say in the partner selection.

In many cases, the marriage arrangements have been made before the bride and groom have reached marriageable age, perhaps even before the son or daughter was born. Brothers sometimes agree to marry their sons and daughters to each other before the children are born, for instance. This form of cousin marriage is not common, especially in the urban areas, but it is a preferred form of marriage in many parts of Islamic society, and found in many traditional segments of the Iranian population.

If the girl's family finds the arrangement acceptable, the discussion quickly turns to the marriage contract, particularly the money to be paid for the bride. Sometimes the amount of the bride-price, or *mahriyeh* in Persian, can be considerable, and in some areas of rural Iran it can amount to several years' wages. The amount of the bride-price depends on the prestige and status of the family, the age of the bride (the younger, the more expensive), and whatever skills or education she might bring to the marriage. The amount of the bride-price also depends on the woman's virtue, since any stain on her honor, or the slightest question about her virginity, will lower the bride-price.

In theory, the bride-price is to compensate the family of the bride for the loss of a daughter, but in fact the real purpose of the bride-price is to pay for the wedding ceremony. In many cases, all or some of the bride-price is not actually paid at the time of the marriage, but is held in reserve in case of a divorce or some other breach of the marriage contract. Bride-price is usually not paid in marriages among westernized Iranians, but this must be specified in the marriage contract.

A man is considered ready to marry when he is able to support a family. In the urban areas among the middle class, readiness to marry may be distinguished when a young man has finished his schooling and secured a satisfactory job. In rural Iran, a man is considered ready to marry when he has inherited enough land or can otherwise support a family. In some areas where the bride-price is high, men may have to work for several years at wage jobs to get enough money to marry, thus postponing the age of marriage. Generally men are in their twenties or older when they marry.

For women, the age of marriage is much younger. In traditional Iran, girls are considered to be of marriageable age when they are able to have children, usually around 15 years old, but often younger. Among the modern middle class, Iranian women usually marry when they have finished their education, usually in their late teens, or in their early twenties if they pursue a college education. Marriage is sometimes later for women in families with several daughters, since daughters are to be married in descending order by age. Younger daughters may have to wait a few extra years while the family marries off the older daughters first.

Before the Islamic revolution in 1979, the Iranian government had raised the legal age of marriage to 18 for females and 21 for males. This was in part to encourage a lower birth rate, but was also designed to increase female school attendance. Since the Islamic revolution, however, the age of marriage has been lowered to 15 years for boys and 13 for girls. While this may appear unreasonably young by Western standards, it is consistent with the actual age of marriage in the more traditional parts of Iranian society, particularly the rural villages, where women marry very young. And marrying at young ages is not unique to Iran. Women in many developing countries marry at very young ages.

There are several consequences of the young age of marriage for women. For one, it increases the birth rate, since women are at risk of conceiving over a longer part of their child-bearing years. Indeed, as will be discussed in Chapter 9, the Iranian birth rate did increase after the Islamic government came to power in 1979. Another consequence of the young age of marriage for women is that it perpetuates the inferiority of women in the marriage relationship.

IRANIAN WEDDINGS

Iranian weddings consist of two parts: the exchange of vows, call the *aghd*, which means bonding, and the reception party, the *arusee*. The exchange of vows is officiated by a member of the clergy, or a professional *aaghed*, who is licensed to perform marriage vows. At the *aghd*, the bride is expected to play hard to get and act disinterested. In the part of the ceremony when the bride is asked if she agrees to the marriage, she oftentimes makes the *aaghed* ask her three times before she agrees, to indicate her coyness (Bagheri).

The *arusee*, the wedding reception, often takes place several months after the exchange of vows, giving the families time to send out invitations and make the arrangements. At the *arusee* food is served, dancing takes place (unless the families are religious), and friends and well-wishers bring flowers for the new couple. Although they were officially married at the exchange of vows, in fact, the couple does not start their life together until after the wedding ceremony.

After the marriage, the new couple usually moves in with the husband's family, which is called **patrilocality.** In modern segments of Iran, this may not involve moving into the actual household of the husband's family, but rather residing in the same compound, village, or neighborhood as the husband's family. While the new wife may keep in touch with her side of the family, she is now part of the groom's extended family. As a new member of the family a new bride is often treated poorly by the groom's mother, although stories of mean mothers-in-law exist in all cultures, and are no doubt exaggerated.

MODERN IRANIAN FAMILY LIFE

Traditional family life is dying in Iran, as it is in the rest of the world. Over the last four decades, a middle class has emerged in Iran for which the traditional family life is no longer desirable or possible. This new class in Iran, as will be discussed later, is largely urbanized and well-educated and eschews many of the traditional modes of Iranian life. This new class is more mobile; the women are more apt to seek higher levels of education and enter careers, and many have received a Western education. They are more apt to live in nuclear families, in single-family housing units; to marry later; to choose their own mate; and to have a more egalitarian relationship between husband and wife. While this new style of Iranian family is the minority, it is growing.

A modern Iranian family of two generations standing in front of a historic mosque in city of Kerman. The women, one of which has a PhD, are veiled, as Iranian women are expected to be in public, but the men are wearing western clothes, including the ubiquitous jeans.

Yet, even among the modern urban middle class, many of the traditional family values still dominate. For instance, while modern couples may make their own marriage arrangements, they still consult with the family elders as a nod to tradition. And Iranian families, modern families included, still value kinship ties and help other family members in need. Among Iranians, both traditional and modern, the elderly are to be respected and, as they become frail, taken care of within the family setting.

SUMMARY AND CONCLUSION

In Iran, family and kinship ties play a significant role in all aspects of life. One's position and status in society are determined by one's kin relations. As a result, the maintenance of family honor and prestige is important. The traditional Iranian family is patrilineal and patriarchal, and the traditional families live in walled compounds in which several nuclear families share communal space, yet have their own areas of privacy. Since family connections are important, marriages in the traditional families are arranged, although that custom is weakening. Finally, the traditional family system is weakening as modern urban living forces accommodations. Despite this, traditional values of family honor and family responsibility remain strong in Iranian society.

CHAPTER 4

Religion in Everyday Life

INTRODUCTION

The Iranian story would not be complete without an understanding of its religious values and beliefs. Perhaps nothing characterizes modern Iranian society as much as the close relationship between the society and Islam. Influences of the pre-Islamic Zoroastrian religion during the Achaemenian and Sassanian cultures may still exist in Iran, but the coming of Islam in the mid-seventh century brought profound changes in Iranian social, spiritual, and religious life. However, Iranians have taken Islam and put their own stamp on it, creating a form of Islam imbued with Iranian personality and character.

Sociologists analyze religion in a number of ways, looking at both the nature of the religion and its role in society. A major distinction sociologists make in analyzing religion is the difference between **sects, cults, denominations,** and **ecclesia.** Ecclesia and denominations are large organized religions, with ecclesia defined as those religions recognized as the state or official religion. There is no ecclesia in the United States, but many denominations. Cults and sects are smaller religious groups, a sect being a small religious group that has broken away from some other religion to renew its spiritual value. Cults are also small groups, often secretive and rebellious, that have either formed a new religion or drastically altered an existing one. Cults and sects often evolve over time to become ecclesia or denominations. Each of these types of religious organization varies by the way it relates to other religious groups and by the values and beliefs of its members. All of these types of religious organizations have been found in Iran.

Religions can play different roles in society. Durkheim (1954), an early sociologist interested in religion, argued that the major role of religion was to provide the social cohesion that holds society together. Another early sociologist, Karl Marx, saw religion as a tool used by the powerful capitalist class to oppress the workers. Other recognized roles of religion in society include providing social control, teaching basic values, providing answers to questions about the meaning of life, and helping people in need. In Iran, we will see that Islam fulfills all of these roles and more.

ISLAM IN IRAN: THE LINE OF THE *IMAMS*

Most Iranians, perhaps over 90 percent, are Moslems belonging to the Shia branch of Islam, usually called the **Twelvers. Shia Islam** developed among early dissenters of Islam in the first three centuries after the death of the Prophet Mohammed in AD 632. The beliefs of the Twelver Shia Moslems differ from the majority of Moslems, called **Sunni Moslems,** in that they believe that the spiritual and temporal leadership of the Moslem community passed from the Prophet Mohammed to his son-in-law Ali and then to 11 of Ali's direct descendants. The Sunnis reject this notion, holding that after Mohammed's death the leadership of Islam passed to Abu Bakr, a contemporary of Mohammed, and subsequently to other leaders selected by the Islamic community. However, the basic religious beliefs of the Sunni and the Shia are similar; they both accept the teachings of the Prophet Mohammed and believe in the Koran, the Islamic holy book. Yet, over the centuries a number of major theological differences have developed between the Shia and the Sunni.

Shia Islam of the Twelver branch has become strongly identified with Iran, since most Shia Moslems are Iranians and Shia theology has been shaped by Iranian thought, but there are Shia Moslems in other countries, particularly those surrounding Iran. There are sizable Shia communities in Syria, Lebanon, Afghanistan, and Iraq and along the rim of the Persian Gulf where Iranian influence can be found. Although there were some Shia in Iran in the early centuries of Islam, most of the Moslems in Iran were probably Sunni until the Safavid dynasty made Shia Islam a state religion in the mid-17th century. At that time in a relatively short period most Iranians converted to the Shia branch, by force or otherwise.

The Shia believe that Ali and the other descendants to the Prophet Mohammed inherited special spiritual powers and thereby are the temporal leaders of the Islamic faith. The Sunni believe that the spiritual powers of the Prophet Mohammed belonged to Mohammed only and were not passed on to his relatives. Not only was Ali the legitimate follower of the Prophet Mohammed in a political sense, but Shia believe that he also inherited the spiritual leadership as well. Shia refer, therefore, to Ali and the 11 descendants that followed him as *Imams.* The word *Imam* is used differently by the Sunni Moslems, who use the word to indicate the person who leads the prayers. In Shia theology an *Imam* has the spiritual ability to interpret the word of God and the hidden meanings of the Koran.

After Ali, who was the first *Imam,* died in AD 662, the line of the *Imams* passed to Ali's descendants, including Ali's sons, Hasan and Hosein, until the line stopped with the 12th *Imam.* The 12th *Imam,* usually called *Sahib al-Zamam* (the lord of time), inherited the *Imam* status when he was only five years old and was never seen again. The Twelvers believe that after living a life on earth, he did not die, but ascended into the spirit world, or the state of occultation, where he awaits God's command to return to earth. In this way, the Twelver version of Shi'ism believes that the line of *Imams* is not finished, only suspended, and by extension, that the spiritual gifts of the Prophet Mohammed are still alive. The hidden *Imam* will eventually return, the Twelvers believe, much like a messiah, at which time he will wage war against the unjust and then establish a period of peace and justice on earth.

As a result of this belief in the blood descendants of the Prophet Mohammed through the lineage of Ali, Ali and his descendants play a major role in the religious belief and practices of Iranians. After Ali's death in AD 672, Mu'awiya became the leader of the Sunni Islamic community and Ali's descendants fell out of power. It fell to Ali's sons to recapture Islam for Ali's descendants. Ali's first son, Hasan, was too weak to be a good leader, but the second son, Hosein, accepted the responsibility of regaining the leadership of the Islamic community. While traveling across the plains of Karbala, now in Iraq, on the 10th of the Islamic month of Moharam in the Islamic year 61 (AD 692) on his way to Kufa to join up with other followers, Hosein and his small band were killed by the army of Yazid, the leader of Islam at that time.

The commemoration of Hosein's death, or the Karbala paradigm, as some scholars have called it (Fischer, 1980), has become the most important event in Shia Islam, as practiced in Iran. Iranians of all walks of life, but particularly in the traditional segments of society, mourn the death of Hosein daily in their prayers, in offtold stories and legends of his martyrdom, in art, and in many other aspects of their daily life. Professional storytellers relate the story of the death of Hosein to gatherings of Iranians who meet weekly or even daily to hear these stories and weep loudly when the details of Hosein's death are recounted. The 10th of the month of Muharram, the day Hosein was killed, is marked throughout Iran and other parts of the Shia world with large public demonstrations of sorrow and remorse, including parades and reenactments of Hosein's death in village squares. At these public demonstrations, men beat themselves with their fists and cut themselves with chains to show their passion and grief for Hosein's death.

The martyrdom of Hosein has also become a symbol for Iranian nationalism and a means of arousing patriotism. Even though Hosein was an Arab, Iranians have reconstructed the story of his death to represent their struggle against the injustice of the world. In the Islamic revolution of 1979 against the shah and his government, the Shia clergy implored the faithful to give their lives "like Hosein gave his life" fighting for Islam. Posters depicted the shah of Iran as Yazid, the ruler who had killed Hosein, to arouse popular sentiment against him.

The martyrdom of Hosein was also used to arouse passions during the bloody war with Iraq from 1980 to 1988. During this terrible war, Iranian youth were exhorted by the Islamic government to give their lives to fight the evil Iraqis like Hosein had done on the plains of Karbala. This symbolism was particularly poignant in the Iran–Iraq war, since the plains of Karbala where Hosein was killed are in what is now eastern Iraq (of course, Iraq did not exist as a country when Hosein was killed).

RELIGIOUS OBLIGATIONS: THE FIVE PILLARS OF ISLAM

As Moslems, Iranians have certain duties or acts they are required to perform. Islam is a religion in which the performance of prescribed acts and rituals and the fulfilling of daily, weekly, and yearly religious obligations are important, in fact, necessary, to be a good Moslem. Certainly the belief in these duties and the faithful performance of these rituals vary by social class and station in Iran. The urbanized secular upper- and middle-class Iranians, while Moslems in spirit, may not adhere to all of the daily rituals of the Islamic faith. In the religious segments of the Iranian society, however, observance of the daily rituals of Islam is strong.

These acts and rituals are codified in a system of Islamic law, called the *Sharia*, which is generally accepted among all Moslems, Shia and Sunni. These laws, which might be better called ethical codes, have been developed by Islamic scholars over the centuries from several sources, including the teachings of the Prophet Mohammed, the words of God spoken by Mohammed in the Koran, and the actions and teachings of other important figures in Islamic history. These laws prescribe what good Moslems should and should not do, and are categorized in ethical importance as (1) obligatory; (2) recommended; (3) indifferent or permissible; (4) reprehensible, but not forbidden; and (5) forbidden (Esposito, 1988: 89). These laws are completely egalitarian and universal; they apply to all Moslems, or for that matter all people, regardless of class, color, gender, or nationality.

These legal obligations are further divided into those that are duties to God, *ibadat*, and those that are duties to the community, *muamalat*. Duties to the community include such things as marriage rules, commercial law, and penal codes. Duties to God include individual obligations such as prayer and fasting. Among the Islamic laws that deal with obligations to God, there are five important duties that are sometimes called the **Five Pillars of Islam.** Although these five duties are no doubt among the most important Islamic laws, their selection is somewhat arbitrary. There are many other duties to God specified in the *Sharia*. Nonetheless the Five Pillars of Islam represent the core of Islamic practice and the five essential obligations that all Moslems must accept and practice.

The Five Pillars of Islam are, of course, rules for Moslems, but they will sound familiar to members of other religions, particularly Jews and Christians. For instance, praying, fasting, and other basic acts of faith are part of Judaism and Christianity and existed in the Middle East before the advent of Islam. Some of the Five Pillars of Islam and other Islamic duties were no doubt borrowed from these religions. Fasting, for instance, may have been borrowed from Jewish tribes that the Prophet Mohammed encountered in Medina, and tithing from the Christian faith. Other duties to God found in the Five Pillars, particularly pilgrimage to Mecca, existed in Arabia before the time of Mohammed.

The first pillar is the **profession of faith,** in Arabic the *Shahada.* Moslems must say in Arabic, "There is no God but the God *(Allah)* and Mohammed is His messenger." The profession of faith is important in two senses. For one, in the phrase "there is no God, but the God" is the affirmation of monotheism, an important part of the Prophet Mohammed's message. The religious beliefs of the Arabian Peninsula in the seventh century contained strong elements of polytheism, although Jewish and Christian communities existed in the area at that time as well. Mohammed saw as one of the main tenets of his prophecy the goal of converting those who believed in polytheism to a true monotheistic faith, which he called Islam. Therefore, to emphasize the strong monotheistic commitment of Islam, the statement of belief in a single God is the first component of the Five Pillars of Islam.

The second part, "and Mohammed is His messenger," affirms the role of Mohammed as a messenger of God. Moslems make a distinction between messengers of God, *rasul,* and prophets of God, *nabi,* messengers being the more important of the two. The mention of Mohammed in the profession of faith does not, however, mean that Moslems do not recognize other messengers and prophets of God. Moslems recognize most of the Old Testament prophets, for instance. In addition, Moslems give the higher status of messenger of God, *rasul,* to Abraham, Moses, and Jesus, as well as Mohammed. Moslems believe, however, that Mohammed was the most important messenger of God, in that he was the last or the "seal" of the prophetic line that began with Abraham.

The profession of faith must be said in Arabic, since Arabic is the language of Islam. Mohammed and his people spoke Arabic, but more importantly it is the language of the Koran, which Moslems believe to be the actual words of God spoken through his messenger Mohammed. Thus the Koran, while it can be translated for secular purposes into other languages, is the true word of God only in Arabic.

A profession of faith is found in most religions, especially other revealed religions in which faith is an important component of religious affiliation. Most Christian or Jewish religious services include at some point a profession of faith.

The second pillar of Islam is **prayer,** *salat* in Arabic or *namaz* in Persian. Moslems must pray five times each day in a prescribed manner. Prayers must be performed facing Mecca, no matter where one is in the world. The times to pray are fixed and are daybreak, noon, midafternoon, sunset, and evening. Moslems can pray wherever they may be, at work, in the fields, on the streets, or at a mosque. Westerners traveling to the Islamic countries for the first time, including Iran, are often surprised to see people stopping wherever they are to kneel and pray at prayer times. Buses pull over at the time of prayer and the passengers pile out to face Mecca and pray to Allah.

Before praying Moslems must ritually cleanse their body, including their hands, face, mouth, and feet, and prepare themselves spiritually. Those praying should put down a mat or rug so as not to soil themselves. Many Moslems carry a small portable mat or rug for prayers. The prayers themselves consist of both bowing and kneeling in the direction of Mecca and touching the forehead to the ground two or four times, depending on the specific prayer and the time of day. The prayer begins with the declaration "God is great," in Arabic *Allah 0 Akbar,* and ends with the peace greeting, "Peace be upon you and the mercy and blessing of God," which is said twice (Esposito, 1988: 91).

The most important prayer service is Friday noon. Friday is the Sabbath in Islam, but unlike in Christianity and Judaism, it is not a day of rest, although most businesses and government agencies close. Many Iranians go to their local mosque for the Friday noon prayer, which is usually accompanied by a sermon, *khutba* in Arabic. The *khutba* can cover any topic, but is often used to rally political support for Islamic causes and to exhort the faithful. At the time of the Islamic revolution in 1979, for instance, the Friday noon sermon at the major Iranian mosques became a forum at which the Islamic leaders launched verbal attacks on the government and incited the faithful to revolt.

The third pillar of Islam is **almsgiving,** or *zakat.* It is the duty of all Moslems to give money for the social welfare of the community. All adult Moslems who are able are expected to give a percentage of their wealth, usually 2.5 percent. This is not regarded as charity but as a religious obligation. In some Moslem countries, *zakat* has become a tax collected by the government, although not in Iran. Tithing and giving to the poor are important parts of Christianity and Judaism as well.

The fourth pillar of Islam is the obligation to **fast,** *sawm,* during the Islamic month of Ramazan (pronounced Rama<u>d</u>an in Arabic). Moslems of good health are expected to refrain from eating, smoking, drinking, and sexual activity from sunrise to sunset during this month. Ramazan is the ninth month in the Islamic calendar. Moslems use a lunar calendar in which months are approximately 27 days long. A lunar year, that is, 12 lunar months, is several days shorter than the solar year. As a result, the month of Ramazan changes seasons through the years, and therefore the length of time of daily fasting changes as the times of sunrise and sunset change. In most Moslem cities, some public signal is given, such as a cannon volley or siren, at sunrise each morning and sunset each evening to tell the faithful when to start and when to stop fasting. Moslems in the United States consult the local paper or watch the weather report on the evening news, which usually lists the times of sunrise and of sunset.

Fasting is a time of reflection and spiritual renewal, to remind those fasting of the frailty of human existence on earth. Those who are sick, traveling, nursing mothers, and the young are not expected to fast.

Fasting, like many of the other duties of Islam, has become common again in Iran after having declined for several decades. Clearly, the reason that fasting and the performance of other religious duties are practiced again in Iran is the return of Islamic fundamentalism to Iran and the control of the country by the Islamic clergy. Gangs of Islamic enforcers patrol the streets of Iran during the month of Ramazan looking for people who do not appear to be fasting, or for restaurants that are open during the day. If offenders are found, they are harassed, fined, or even arrested. The result, as with the veiling of women, is to create a double life among secular Iranians or non-Moslems in Iran between the public and private spheres of their lives. In public they must appear pious, to be obeying the Islamic laws, but in the privacy of their homes they may live quite differently. Middle-class Iranians tell of rubbing dirt on their lips when they go out in public during the month of Ramazan so that their lips will look dry and people will think that they are fasting.

The fifth pillar is the **pilgrimage** to Mecca, the *hajj* in Arabic. All Moslems who are able must make the pilgrimage to the holy city of Mecca, now in Saudi Arabia, during the month of pilgrimage, *Dhu al-Hajja,* at least once during their lifetime. The trip to Mecca is, in fact, beyond the means of most Iranians, except the rich. As a result, most Iranian Moslems never make the pilgrimage to Mecca. But about two million Moslems from around the world each year do make the pilgrimage. While in Mecca, the pilgrims perform a series of ritual acts that in part reenact the life of the Prophet Mohammed. To many Iranians the pilgrimage to Mecca is the most important religious event in their lives, and upon returning they take the title of *hajji,* meaning "one who has done the pilgrimage." There are lesser pilgrimages to other holy cities of Islam as well.

With so many pilgrims at one time and because of their special needs, the pilgrimage has put an enormous strain on Saudi Arabia. Each of the two million pilgrims must slaughter a goat or sheep while in Mecca, for instance, and many Moslems make the pilgrimage when they are sick and old. As a result Saudi Arabia has put a limit on how many pilgrims may come from each Islamic country, and this has caused tensions between Iran and Saudi Arabia.

Beyond its religious and spiritual significance, the pilgrimage once played an important role in the economy and politics of the Islamic world. The *hajj* was a yearly event in which all of the important people in Islam would gather to trade information and goods, including slaves, and to make political decisions. Even now, because Islam is made up of different branches, some with quite antagonistic beliefs toward other Moslems, the pilgrimage can be a time of conflict. Recently Iranian pilgrims at Mecca held a demonstration to protest their treatment by the government of Saudi Arabia. This demonstration resulted in a riot causing a number of deaths in the holy city. As a result, Saudi Arabia has tried to limit the number of pilgrims allowed each year from Iran and keeps a very close eye on those that come.

Pilgrimages to holy places are a part of other religions as well. The crusades were holy pilgrimages. Every year thousands of European and American Christians flock to the Holy Land to see where Jesus lived and preached.

There are other important acts of faith in Islam. One other, sometimes called the sixth pillar, is the *jihad*, or the holy struggle. In modern usage, *jihad* has come to mean a holy war, and the term has been used by a number of militant Islamic groups, including the Iranian clergy during the revolution in 1979, to mean a military battle. In its more general meaning, however, *jihad* refers to the obligation of all Moslems to lead a virtuous life and to do God's work.

In addition to the Five Pillars, there are additional religious obligations and practices specific to the Shia Moslems. Important among these is the observance of the month of Moharram and commemoration of the death of Hosein. Other religious obligations are pilgrimages to the shrines of the Shia *Imams* and their relatives. The eighth *Imam* is buried in the Iranian city of Mashad and his sister Fatima in the Iranian holy city of Qom. Shrines of lesser relatives of the *Imams* are in Shiraz and in the city of Rey on the southern outskirts of Tehran. Throughout Iran there are smaller shrines of the descendants of the *Imams*, called *imamzadehs* in Persian, where local Iranians visit and ask for spiritual guidance. Many Iranians believe that the *Imams*, and therefore their descendants, have special powers to intercede with God to heal a sick child, bless a marriage, or grant some other special wish.

THE ISLAMIC HIERARCHY: *MUJTAHIDS*, *SAYYIDS*, AND *MULLAHS*

Most Moslems maintain that there is no clergy as such in Islam. By this they mean two things. In the institutional sense, Islam is not represented by a single institutional entity, such as the Catholic Church, with a pope, cardinals, bishops, priests, and so on. Islam, therefore, has no single leader, nor is it organized into one or a few institutions for whom most Islamic teachers, scholars, or preachers work. The second reason for saying that Islam has no clergy is in the spiritual sense. In Islam, each person stands on his or her own before God, without the intercession or help of a priest. Moslems pray on their own, for instance, even when they are with others. There may be a person who stands in the front of the congregation and leads the prayer at a mosque, but he is only initiating the prayer service; persons must recite their prayers on their own.

However, beyond these two meanings, to say that there is no Islamic clergy is inaccurate, especially in Iran. In Iran there is a distinct clergy, called the *ulama*, meaning those learned in Islamic law, who play a much greater role in interpreting Islam for the faithful than in the other branches of Islam. The *ulama* form a social and religious class in Iran with special rights and statuses. The *ulama* have played an important political and spiritual role in Iran going back to the time of the Safavids in the 16th century, but their impact on society is at its greatest in modern Iran. The *ulama* usually have had religious training and are generally recognized for their religious wisdom.

The *ulama* are in turn organized into hierarchical groups according to their religious learning and wisdom. The highest religious authorities in Iran are called, as a group, *mujtahids,* which means interpreters of Islamic law. They are given high status in Iran and have political and religious authority. They act as leaders in the Islamic community in religious issues and resolve disputes that arise over the interpretation of Islamic law. They were the vanguard of the Islamic revolution in 1979 and now constitute the ruling elite in Iran. The *mujtahids* are easily recognized with their full beards, their white turban, and the *aba,* a loose sleeveless brown cloak.

Mujtahids gain their status by completing a lengthy and rigorous course of study in Islamic law and theology at Islamic seminaries, called *madrasehs,* found mostly in the holy Shia cities of Qom and Mashad in Iran, and Najaf in Iraq. Of equal importance to becoming a *mujtahid* is the informal recognition in the Islamic community, particularly the *ulama,* that one has become truly learned in Islamic law and theology. Very few seminarians ever make it to the level of *mujtahid,* and those who do are usually over the age of 30.

A few *mujtahids* become particularly well known and develop a large following. Beginning in the 20th century, these *mujtahids* have been given the title of *ayatollah,* which means the "sign of God." Like the title of *mujtahid,* the title *ayatollah* is conferred by reputation and does not indicate an official rank in an organization. Nonetheless, *ayatollahs* have tremendous power and prestige in Iran. There are about 50 *ayatollahs* in Iran all over the age of 50. Most occupy positions as the heads of prestigious *madrasehs,* or Islamic seminaries. Among the *ayatollahs,* a few may gain such high religious status that they achieve almost universal authority over religious issues in Iran and are given the title of *Ayatollah al-Ozma,* or the grand *Ayatollah.* Such authority was given to Ayatollah Khomeini during the Islamic revolution, as well as to six other *ayatollahs.*

There are other religious figures in Iran. Mentioned before are people who claim to be descendants of the Prophet Mohammed through the family of Ali. These people are given the title of *sayyid* and are given some status, particularly in rural Iran, as having special spiritual qualities as direct blood descendants of the line of the *Imams.* Being a *sayyid,* however, is different from being a *mujtahid.* On the one hand, being a *sayyid* is an **ascribed status,** a status that society confers to people because of their lineage, not something that they have accomplished themselves. On the other hand, being a *mujtahid* is an **achieved status,** a status that society has given to those who have achieved exceptional learning and wisdom. As a result in modern Iran, *sayyids* have less status than *mujtahids.* However, it is not uncommon that some of the leading *mujtahids* are also *sayyids.* Ayatollah Khomeini is an example. In addition, since inherited characteristics spread exponentially with each generation, there are tens of thousands of people in Iran who are, or claim to be, *sayyids*. Therefore, being a *sayyid* is not necessarily a title of great honor in Iran anymore, although in some other Shia countries, particularly among Afghan Shia, it remains an important title.

Much of the discussion to this point has been about the Islamic clergy at the national level. At the local level, particularly in the villages where most Iranians once lived and where many Iranians still live, there are local Islamic leaders usually called *mullahs* or *akhunds*. *Mullahs* are the equivalent to the village priest in rural parishes. They lead the local prayers, settle local disputes, perform marriage ceremonies, bury the dead, and instruct the village children in religious subjects. They are usually self-selected: *mullahs* are usually local people who have taken it upon themselves to take on this role. They are not assigned to the village by the Islamic organization, since there is no Islamic organization. Some may have studied at a religious school, or *madraseh*; others are self-taught. Many have inherited the position from their fathers. Many village *mullahs* in Iran, especially in remote areas, are only semiliterate, being able to recite the Koran, but not able to read otherwise. In many cases their knowledge of Islam is rudimentary and faulty, and their interpretation of Islamic law crude and heavy-handed. These local *mullahs* may receive some money for their services, but usually they must also work at farming or labor to support themselves.

In Iran and other parts of the Middle East, village *mullahs* are held in some contempt by urbanites who see them as country bumpkins. They are the butt of many jokes and stories regarding their stupidity, sexual preference, and understanding of Islam. This view of the village *mullah* also reflects a deeper rift between the urban and village worlds in Iran, and the general contempt that the urban middle- and upper-class Iranians have for villagers.

One version of the village *mullah*, however, is a person who is dumb like a fox. There is a collection of fictional stories about a village *mullah*, named Mullah Nasruddin, that all Iranians know and tell to their children. In these stories Mullah Nasruddin does something that appears stupid, but in fact turns out to be quite clever, usually turning the tables on the pompous or upper class. The Mullah Nasruddin tales, or related stories of stupid, but smart, rural priests, are found in all of the Islamic societies.

RELIGIOUS INSTITUTIONS: MOSQUES, SCHOOLS, SHRINES, AND ENDOWMENTS

Mosques

While there is no single overearching religious organization in Iran, there are a number of specific religious institutions around which religious life is organized. These include religious places of worship, religious schools, religious shrines, and religious endowments that provide the financial support for these activities. Historically, the single most important religious institution in Iran for the average Iranian is the mosque, *masjid* in Persian. The mosque is the place of worship for most Iranians, equivalent in some ways to the church in Christianity or the synagogue in Judaism. In most towns and cities, mosques play a dominant role in the life of the men, who assemble at the mosque for Friday noon congregational prayers. People, including non-Moslems, come to the mosque at other times to meditate or pray, since they are usually quiet and inspirational settings. Foreigners are generally welcome into Islamic mosques, even during prayers, as long as they follow mosque etiquette, which includes, among other things, removing one's shoes and, of course, acting reverential. Iranian mosques, like American churches, play other roles as well. In the poorer parts of the cities, food may be distributed from the mosques. During the Islamic revolution, mosques were used to recruit demonstrators, to pass out revolutionary literature, and, in general, to organize and manage the revolution as it unfolded.

Mosques are largely an urban institution and generally not found in villages. As in other areas of the Middle East, most Iranian cities feature a large mosque at the center of the city's central square. In the Iranian cities of Qom, Isfahan, and Mashad, for instance, the central mosques are large, beautiful, ornate buildings with colorful blue tile work, golden domes, and open courtyards. The mosques have a number of interesting architectural features that reflect their religious function. For one, Moslems must pray facing Mecca and, therefore, mosques must be located so that the pulpit, *minbar*, is aligned in the direction of Mecca. It is not unusual to see mosques built at an angle different from the buildings around it.

It is important also that the mosques have minarets from which Moslems are called to prayer five times a day by the *muezzin*, or caller to prayer. Historically, the *muezzin* would climb one of the minarets five times each day and call the faithful to pray. Now in Iran, and in most Islamic countries, electronic loudspeakers have been put at the top of the minarets so that the *muezzin* can perform his daily duties from the ground.

The elaborate geometrical designs seen on the larger mosques, usually carried out in blue tile, are also a result of religions prescriptions. In Islam, the depiction of human or animal form is forbidden. As a result, geometrical design and calligraphy are used in mosque architecture. In contrast, European church architecture often features statues and stained-glass windows depicting scenes with human and animal forms.

Mosques are locally owned and organized, except for some large mosques that are supported by the government. Local patrons usually donate money for the building and upkeep of their local mosque. The *mullah*, or *akhund*, who leads the prayers in the mosque and directs other mosque activities is usually locally hired. His salary and upkeep are contributed by local patrons. When a new leader is needed, a delegation of local members of the mosque travel to an Islamic seminary, usually in the city of Qom or Mashad, and select another leader for their mosque.

Madrasehs and *Maktabs*

Another important religious institution in Iran is the Islamic seminary, or *madraseh* in Persian. *Madrasehs* are the equivalent to the Christian seminary or the Jewish yeshiva. They played an important historical role in the development of Shia theology and law and the training of religious scholars. The *madrasehs* are found mostly in the Shia holy cities of Qom, Mashad, and Najaf in Iraq and are associated with noted Shia scholars, usually *ayatollahs,* who have developed a following, although several *ayatollahs* may teach at one *madraseh.* There are older *madrasehs* that are supported through endowments and are not associated with a particular Islamic theologian.

While the *madraseh* played an important role as both a religious institution and an educational institution of higher learning historically, it has become less fashionable for students to study at them in recent times. For many centuries the *madrasehs* in Iran, as in most of the Middle East, were the only form of higher education available, as were the Catholic seminaries in medieval Europe. They taught not only Islamic theology, but also medicine, science, and geography. It was through the *madraseh* system that much of the knowledge of Greek and Roman civilization was collected and taught, and eventually passed on to Europe. As with the European seminaries, however, the *madraseh* has been bypassed by modern secular education. By 1979, 20 modern universities had been built in Iran, and most Iranian students preferred the opportunities afforded by a modern education, and enrollment in the *madrasehs* declined. By the time of the Islamic revolution, the *madraseh* students had become a small minority in Iran and restricted to those interested in Islamic theology (Fischer, 1980).

The revolution of 1979 did much to revive the status of the *madraseh.* Enrollments again grew as the study of Islamic theology regained popularity. Many of the *ayatollahs* who taught at the *madrasehs* became the new leaders of Iran, and their new status attracted new students to their schools. Nonetheless, the *madraseh* students remain a minority, with most post-secondary students preferring a university education in one of the Iranian universities or abroad.

There are also religious primary schools, called *maktabs.* These schools offered secular and religious training and were the only schools for primary-age children until modern secular education came to Iran at the end of the 19th century. *Maktabs* had largely died out, particularly, in the major cities, by the 1960s, but continued to exist as private schools for those who specifically wanted a religious education. After the Islamic revolution, the government desecularized the public schools and merged the public school system with the *maktabs.*

Shrines

There are over 1,000 religious shrines in Iran, some crumbling in decay and others large modern complexes of tombs, libraries, mosques, and soup kitchens for the poor. Among the sights visitors to Iran will see when driving through the countryside are the numerous local shrines to local saints covered with colorful ribbons and flags. Most of the 1,000 plus shrines are *imamzadehs*, that is, the tomb of someone who was a descendant of the *Imams*.

The most important of these shrines is that of Imam Reza, the eighth *Imam*, who is buried in Mashad. This shrine is considered the holiest in Iran. The complex includes a library, a hospital, a museum, a dispensary, and several mosques around a series of courtyards leading to the tomb of Imam Reza. Several thousand pilgrims visit the shrine each day, and free meals are served to as many as 1,000 people daily. People who make the pilgrimage are called *mashdi* and awarded some status in traditional Iranian society. The shrine is supported by a wealthy endowment. Other important shrines are in Qom, Shiraz, and Rey.

While the mosques play a central role in the religious life of males in Iran, shrines are also important to women. Women visit the shrines as mothers or wives to pray for a sick child or a departed husband. Visitors tie small pieces of colorful cloth to the outer surface of the shrine or to nearby trees as a remembrance for a lost loved one or for good fortune.

Islamic Endowments

Behind the scenes in all religious institutions in any society are the financial pillars by which the religious organizations receive the money they need to operate. One of the ways in which the activities of Islamic organizations, including the schools, shrines, and mosques, are financed is through a traditional form of financial endowment call the *waqf*. As with Americans, it is not uncommon for wealthy Iranians to leave a piece of property or other income-producing assets to a religious institution for perpetuity. Through the *waqf* endowments, many religious institutions, and the religious leaders that control them, have amassed a considerable fortune over the centuries, primarily in the accumulation of agricultural lands. The Islamic organizations in Iran are therefore among the largest landholders in Iran. As a result, the clergy violently opposed the land reform provisions of the Mohammed Reza Shah's White Revolution, since it would have given much of the *waqf* lands that support the religious organizations to the peasants who work the fields.

ISLAM IN IRANIAN LIFE: TWO IRANS

We have seen that at its roots Islam has much in common with Christianity and Judaism, despite dramatic differences on the surface. Iranians pray, fast, mourn, praise God, and participate in their religious activities much as do people of other religious faiths. Islam is a faith that grew out of the Judeo-Christian tradition, and Moslems are conscious of their ties to these religions. Also, we have seen that although Iranians are Moslems following the teachings of Mohammed and the main tenets of the Islamic faith, they have taken a branch of Islam, called Shi'ism, and have made it their own, imbuing it with a Persian personality and making it into a statement of Iranian passion and nationalism. It is the passion of the Shia Islamic tradition, with the martyrdom of Imam Hosein at the center, that has fueled much of the fervor and zeal of the recent Islamic revolution in Iran and motivated Iranian youth to give their lives in the war with Iraq.

As in other countries, the strength of religious belief and the participation in religious activities vary by one's position in society. Unlike in most other countries, however, this difference in religious conviction, particularly after the Islamic revolution in 1979, has created two Irans: a religious Iran and a secular Iran. In the religious Iran, Islamic values and practices are zealously observed, and in secular Iran traditional Islamic values and practices are less important and infrequently practiced. These two Irans live side by side, but are dramatically different and hostile toward each other.

To many Iranians, particularly those in rural areas or in the poor areas of the cities where recent rural immigrants now live, ties to traditional Islamic values and practices are strong and may have grown even stronger since the Islamic revolution. The revolutionary Islam preached by the Islamic clergy resonates with this Iran's view of the world. These lower-class Iranians have been recently uprooted by the forces of modernization that have thrown them off their lands or out of a job. They resent the secularized version of Iran that they saw coming under the shah and his government. Crowded into the poorer parts of cities, or left in impoverished villages where their land had been taken over by wealthy urban landlords, they find in the teaching of the Islamic clergy a message they like. Not only do the clergy preach against the corrupting and evil influences of modernization and Westernization, but in Islam they also find the message of egalitarianism and ultimate salvation. In the eyes of *Allah* they are as good as anybody else, they are told, and if they believe in *Allah* and his Prophet Mohammed, they will have peace. The role of Islam in the lives of the traditional lower classes, who constitute the majority of the Iranian population, has increased in the last two decades. Their belief in Islam has strengthened and become more zealous, even as their economic and social condition has declined. These people were the foot soldiers of the Islamic revolution and, in a way, it was their revolution. They are now the followers of the Islamic clergy that rule Iran. This is their Iran.

The other Iran is the secular upper and middle classes of Iranians in the larger cities. These people have often received a modern secular education and ties to traditional Islamic values and practices have weakened over the decades. This does not mean that these Iranians are not Moslems; most would say they are. But to them, Islam offers general guidelines of life, and they have less interest in the specific rules of Islam such as daily prayer, fasting, and particularly the prescribed veiling of women and the separation of the sexes. These upper- and middle-class Iranians would prefer to see a more secularized Iran, where religious practices and beliefs are personal choices, not governmental edicts. This Iran did well under the shah's government, and, while they may not have supported his repressive tactics, they preferred the open religious atmosphere of that period in which the Islamic rules were not enforced and non-Islamic behavior was tolerated. These Iranians are not followers of the present Islamic government; quite the contrary, they fear and loath it.

There are also several hundred thousand Iranians who are not Moslems, including Jews, Christians, Zoroastrians, and Baha'is. In a country where Islamic values are strong and Islamic rules zealously followed, the existence of non-Moslem communities is at times difficult. Most non-Moslem communities have made their peace with Islam, but they must abide by Islamic codes of behavior in public and always be alert not to offend Islamic sensibilities, even by accident. Some groups, like the Baha'is, are persecuted in modern Iran, because they are seen as enemies of Islam.

Many hundreds of thousands of middle- and upper-class Iranians have fled Iran before, during, and after the Islamic revolution, most to Europe and the United States. Those who stayed live in fear, and live lives in which their public and private worlds are quite different. In public, they appear to adhere to the practices of Islam in their dress and actions. However, many of the private hobbies or interests they had before the Islamic revolution, such as listening to Western music, watching Western movies, drinking alcohol, or attending gatherings with men and women present, are now forbidden in Iran. The Islamic police patrol the streets looking for people who are not observing Islamic practices. In private, even in secret, they may continue these activities, but the fear of being caught is always present.

Islam did not create the two Irans; the split has been growing since the 19th century. But the Islamic revolution in Iran has made the split between the two Irans more obvious and, for many Iranians, more painful. The Iranians who were on the top of society are now on the bottom, and those on the bottom are now on the top. Or so it appears.

CHAPTER 5

The Iranian Political System

INTRODUCTION

Politics is the study of "who gets what, and how" (Lasswell, 1936). In other words, political systems are based on **power,** meaning the ability to control others, even those who might not want to be controlled. Power may, and often does, derive from brute force or by threat, but the power on which most governments depend is usually called **authority,** institutionalized power that is generally accepted as legitimate by most of the people over whom it is exercised. The nature and origins of authority were, and continue to be, of great interest to sociologists, since on it rest the foundations of government. That is, all governments rest on the question of the legitimacy of their authority, the question of how the use of authority by the political institutions is accepted by the people as being proper and appropriate. The means by which authority is used determines the nature of the political structure.

One of the earliest sociologists, Max Weber (1947), describes three types of authority. **Traditional authority** is power that has been gained through traditional means, most often through heredity. This is most prevalent in pre-industrial societies in which ruling families or clans dominate and positions of leadership are passed on by traditional rules of patrilineal descent. The last shah of Iran was a traditional leader, as were most of the rulers of Iran before him, and the monarchies of medieval Europe were based on traditional authority. Traditional leaders usually embrace traditional values and resist change. However, as societies modernize, people are less willing to give authority to traditional leaders, and in the last several decades most of the world monarchies have disappeared, including the Iranian monarchy.

The second kind of authority is called **charismatic authority.** This is authority that leaders acquire because of the power or persuasiveness of their personalities. Jesus was a charismatic leader, as was Ayatollah Khomeini. Charismatic leaders often appear during times of societal change or crisis, and often lead revolutions or bring about dramatic social change. Charismatic authority is most often unstable in the long run, because it depends on the power of a single person. When that person is gone, the charismatic authority goes with him. The challenge of institutionalizing charismatic authority after the charismatic leader has left the scene is often faced by post-revolutionary governments, as was Iran after the death of Ayatollah Khomeini in 1989.

The last form of authority recognized by Max Weber is **legal authority,** authority legitimized by people's belief in the laws of the government. This type of authority can exist only when there is a legitimate government that is accepted by most of the people, and where constitutional restraints and processes exist. With legal authority, obedience is to a system, not to a person or, for that matter, to a tradition. Leaders with legal authority are elected or appointed according to regularized governmental processes. The modern leaders of Iran have been elected or appointed according to the Iranian constitution and are therefore legitimate in Iranian society.

IRANIAN POLITICS

The Iranian political system, like most phenomena in Iran, is complicated and complex. To the Western eye, the Iranian government, led by men in robes and beards, and based on Islamic tenets and laws, appears to be more akin to medieval Europe, based on traditional authority, than to a modern country. Yet, as we will learn, the Iranian system is anything but old. The creation of a system of government in which religion plays a key role, but that is modern in other respects, has required an imaginative blending of old and new forms and systems.

The political system of Iran must also be understood in the light of the revolution in 1979. Revolutions create their own reality and momentum. Much of the political activity in Iran in the last 20 years is a reaction to or a consequence of the forces released by the Islamic revolution that turned Iranian society upside down and brought a new ruling elite to power. Iran has had to create a functioning government and a new constitution in a short period to replace the traditional political system of the monarchy and the charismatic heroes of the revolutionary period. This process is still incomplete.

Finally, Iranian politics needs to be seen in its historical perspective. Before 1979, Iran had the politics of royalty, an almost absolute monarch to whom personal loyalty was demanded, with little political dissent allowed. Now Iran has the politics of revolutionary zeal and Islamic ideology in which loyalty to the Islamic cause is demanded. Political dissent is still greatly limited in the post-1979 Iran, but one factor has changed. In the aftermath of the Islamic revolution, the people of Iran now know that they can change the system.

POLITICS BEFORE 1979

The Iranian government of Mohammed Reza Shah, who ruled from 1941 to 1979, and for that matter the governments of all of the shahs of Iran going back to the beginning of the Safavid dynasty in the 16th century, had four characteristics: reliance on the personal power of the shah, lack of constitutional restraint (constitutions are a modern development, and therefore constitutional issues do not apply to the earlier periods), the prohibition of political dissent, and the lack of human rights.

Personal Power

The authority of the Iranian governmental structure up to 1979 rested in the personal authority of the shah himself. Although surrounded by a large political elite, the core of the elite was the shah and his immediate family. One's position in the government was directly related to one's distance from the shah. There were periods in the rule of many of the shahs of Iran, including Mohammed Reza, when others, often prime ministers, became important and even briefly assumed power, but ultimately the central power of the shah was upheld. This rule of personality meant that little could happen in Iran without the direct knowledge and approval of the monarch. As a result, the political system was based on absolute allegiance to the throne, and not to the government or the country in a larger sense. The average Iranian was therefore passive in regard to political participation.

This personal form of government was ultimately incapable of meeting the demands of a modern country for several reasons. For one, the demands of modern government are simply too complex and require too much sophisticated knowledge for a single person, or even a small group of people, to command. Modern bureaucracies are much better at rationalizing and organizing the operations of government than a single ruler and his clique. In addition, the 20th century has brought the demand for participatory democracy. People in most countries, especially the members of newly emerging middle classes, want to participate in the decisions of the country. In this era of human history, monarchies have largely died out, or have been made into constitutional figureheads.

The Lack of Constitutional Restraint

The second characteristic of the Iranian governments before 1979 is that they operated in the absence of a formal constitution to which the government was truly accountable. At the time of the Islamic revolution, Iran was in name a constitutional monarchy, based on the constitution of 1906, but this constitution was largely ignored by Mohammed Reza Shah's government and his father's before him. The 1906 constitution was developed as a compromise between the secular nationalist forces and the Islamic clergy at that time. Based on a European model, its goal was to create a modern government with an elected parliament that would limit the power of the shah. The 1906 constitution also asserted the importance of Islamic ideology in the actions and decisions of the government. The constitution said little about human rights, and in fact placed limits on individual freedoms insofar as they conflicted with Islamic morality. Over the years, Iranian parliaments have tried to reassert their constitutional mandate, at times with temporary success, but the government of the shah overruled the parliamentary actions as the shah pleased.

Prohibition of Political Dissent

The third characteristic of the government of Mohammed Reza Shah was that it tolerated almost no political dissent or opposition. At the time of the fall of the shah, there was one "official" opposition party, *Rastakhiz*. There were other political parties in Iran and many political thinkers, but they were generally not allowed to operate openly or to engage in meaningful public political dialogue. As a result many parties operated clandestinely, and their leaders were periodically arrested or detained. The clandestine parties, most of which had been at one time legal in Iran, included political orientations from the far left, the middle, and the far right. Among the best known was the **National Front,** a centrist coalition made of democratically inclined mainstream political parties and represented by members of the power elite; the **Tudeh** party, a Marxist party founded in 1941 with close ties to the Soviet Union; the **Fadaiyan,** an independent Marxist guerrilla organization; and the **Mojahedin-e Khalq,** a leftist guerrilla organization that combined Islamic and left-wing ideology. All of these parties would play a role in the revolution, but under the rule of Mohammed Reza Shah they were not allowed to operate and their members were rounded up from time to time and jailed.

Lack of Human Rights

Finally, the rule of the shah was characterized by the lack of human rights. During the reign of Mohammed Reza Shah, Iranian citizens could be arrested without trial or reason. The secret police had supreme authority to hold and detain people, and Iranians generally learned to keep their mouths shut and their heads down. This is not to say that there was no political discussion, or that Iranians lived in terror all of the time. Rather, Iranian citizens always knew during the rule of Mohammed Reza Shah that, if the government decided to crack down and arrest people, there was no recourse.

THE ISLAMIC IRANIAN GOVERNMENT

When the Islamic leadership took over Iran following the revolution in 1979, it faced the task of creating a new government based on Islamic law.

FIGURE 5-1

The Power of the *Faqih*

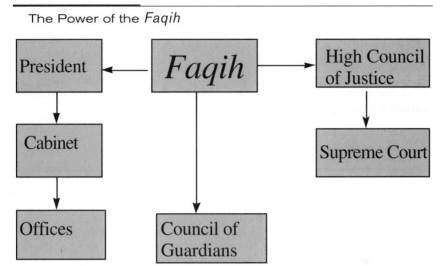

Source: Adapted from Metz, 1987, p. 198.

Ayatollah Khomeini had first begun to contemplate such a government while in exile in Iraq in the 1970s and had published a tract on the topic. Although the details of what such a government would look like were not worked out at the time, Ayatollah Khomeini's idea was to create a governmental structure in which the Shia clergy would have ultimate control over the government through the concept of a *velayat-e faqih*, or the guardianship of the religious jurists. After the Islamic revolution in 1979, a special assembly of experts was formed to write a constitution based on these concepts. The constitution was written and ratified in late 1979.

In part, the new constitution is based on the French constitution written under Charles de Gaulle in 1958. The 1979 Iranian constitution calls for a strong president elected every four years; a parliament elected once every four years; a judiciary of Islamic judges appointed by the Islamic leader; and a prime minister and cabinet, appointed by the president and approved by the parliament. The office of prime minister was eliminated in the constitutional revisions in the summer of 1989. What makes the new Iranian constitution Islamic is the central role played by the Islamic clergy through the position of the *faqih*, or supreme Islamic jurist, and the Council of Guardians. The Council of Guardians consists of six Islamic jurists, experts on Islamic law, and six laypeople who are experts on constitutional law. The supreme leader selects the six Islamic jurists and consults with the parliament on the six laymen. The council's role is to examine the actions of the parliament and to veto bills that are viewed as against Islamic tenets.

The *faqih* is the centerpiece of the new governmental structure (see Figure 5-1). This person is the most powerful person in Iran and controls virtually all aspects of the government. The new constitution named Aya-tollah Khomeini *faqih* for life and specified the process by which a succes-sor would be named. Ayatollah Khomeini died in 1989, and the present *faqih* is Ayatollah Khamenie, who has also been named *faqih* for life. The duties of the *faqih* include appointing the Council of Guardians, appoint-ing the chief judges, appointing the chief of staff of the military, and ap-proving candidates for president. In addition, the *faqih* can dismiss the president if he is impeached by the parliament. He is the supreme ruler of Iran, in fact, but unlike the role of the shahs before him, his role is more to advise and approve rather than to run the day-to-day operation of the government.

CONTROLLING THE REVOLUTIONARY TURMOIL

The sociologist Theda Skocpol (1979, 1982) makes a distinction between **political revolutions** and **social revolutions.** Political revolutions occur when the governing structure of a country is overthrown but the social structure stays intact. The American revolution was a political revolution. Social revolutions occur when there are "rapid, basic transformations of a country's state and class structure, and of its dominant ideology" (Skocpol, 1982: 265). Social revolutions lead to more profound change in society, and, as a result, it takes more effort and time to put the society back to-gether and to restore order and function after the revolution itself is over.

The Iranian revolution of 1979 was a social revolution, and it is now two decades old. Yet the forces unleashed by the revolution continue to buffet Iran. The new post-revolutionary government has withstood a number of serious challenges, including the impeachment of the first president; the assassination of the second president, a prime minister, several members of the cabinet, and several members of parliament; an effort to overthrow the government by armed opposition; an invasion by Iraq followed by a bloody war; and the death of its charismatic leader Ayatollah Khomeini in 1989.

All revolutions create strong social and political forces that, once unleashed, are very difficult to bring under control. In Iran this process is still going on. This process has four stages, each dealing with distinct po-litical issues. The first stage after the revolution was marked by the col-lapse of the shah's government and the creation of a provisional govern-ment. With the shah defeated, the revolution turned inward. Iranians of all walks of life, buoyed by the success of the revolution, turned from the national level and brought the revolutionary zeal to the places where they worked, lived, or studied. Hundreds of *komitehs* (Persian adaptation of the French word *comité,* here meaning revolutionary cell or group) sprang up in neighborhoods, factories, mosques, schools, and universi-ties in all parts of Iran. In the name of the Islamic revolution, these *komitehs* seized control of their work or living places from the former au-thorities and began to mete out justice and punishment as they saw fit, uncontrolled by any central authority. The provisional government tried to restore order, but these *komitehs* were reluctant to give power back to the central government. The Islamic leaders were also hesitant to curb these revolutionary groups, partly out of fear, since these *komitehs* represented the vanguard of the revolution. Some revolutionary leaders, in fact, argued at that time that a return to a centralized bureaucracy was destructive and that the Islamic revolutionary goals were better served by the local representation of people in numerous local revolutionary organizations. Stage one came to an end when a group of radical Islamic students from several universities overran the American Embassy in Tehran in November 1979 and took a number of Americans hostage. This dramatic event galvanized the world, including Iran, and the result was that the official government lost all control of the country to the revolutionary groups. The provisional government was unable to regain control of Iran and was eventually forced to resign.

The second stage of the revolution began when the new Islamic constitution was written and ratified in December 1979 and the first president, Bani Sadr, was elected in January 1980. Bani Sadr was a confidant of Ayatollah Khomeini and had been with him in exile in Paris, but he was not a member of the high Islamic clergy. He was in fact a secular nationalist strongly influenced by French and leftist thought. He was perhaps an unlikely selection as the first president of an Islamic government, but Ayatollah Khomeini supported him. However, he was resented by the Islamic leaders who had fought in the revolution. Most of the stalwarts of the revolution were elected to the first Islamic parliament, and this first parliament clashed with the new president on who should rule the country, the newly elected parliament controlled by the fundamentalist clergy or the newly elected president backed by more secular leaders. By 1981, the clergy in the parliament had won, and they voted to impeach Bani Sadr after he had served only 18 months in office. He was soon forced to flee Iran and was later killed in Paris.

The third stage of the Islamic revolution was the bloodiest and was called the "reign of terror." By 1981 it was clear that the Islamic clergy had seized control of Iran and other political groups who had participated in the revolution had been pushed aside. These groups, including particularly the *Mojahedin-e Khalq,* or People's Struggle, resented not playing a role in a government they felt they had helped create and began a series of terrorist attacks aimed at leaders of the Islamic government. On June 28, 1981, the *Mojahedin-e Khalq* bombed the headquarters of the Islamic Republic Party, killing at least 70 Islamic leaders. Then on August 30, 1981, they bombed the prime minister's office, killing, among others, the president and the prime minister. (It was never proved that the *Majahedin-e Khalq* did the bombing.)

The Islamic government quickly retaliated by carrying out mass arrests and executions. Islamic vigilantes went from house to house arresting anyone whom they suspected of being a supporter of the *Mojahedin-e Khalq.* Civil rights were suspended and revolutionary courts set up. As many as 50 people per day were tried in summary fashion and immediately executed when found guilty. The reign of terror officially ended in December 1982 when Ayatollah Khomeini instructed the courts to reinstitute legal process, to protect the rights of citizens from unfair trial, and banned such practices as forcible entry and arrest without judicial orders.

The fourth stage of the revolutionary aftermath began in December 1982 and continues today. This stage is marked by a gradual return to normal governmental functions and the harnessing of the revolutionary zeal into institutionalized channels. In 1982 the Iranian universities were reopened after having been closed for several years. Parliamentary elections took place without incident in 1985, and in general Iran began to return to more normal functioning. A crisis occurred in 1989 when Ayatollah Khomeini died, but by this time the Iranian Islamic government was fully in control and his successor was named without great turmoil or bloodshed.

HUMAN RIGHTS UNDER THE ISLAMIC REPUBLIC

Although conditions in Iran may have improved since the period of the reign of terror in the early 1980s, serious human rights violations are still common. Amnesty International's report on Iran (1995) lists a number of basic human rights violations in the Islamic Republic. These include the detention of political prisoners for long periods of time in poor conditions. As in most cases of political detention, families have little or no information about what has happened to a loved one. Those arrested are often critics of the government. They are held without trial, sometimes for more than 10 years, and when there is a trial, they are usually charged with the vaguely worded "activities against the Islamic Republic" (Amnesty International, 1995: 4). The trials are often summary in nature and the accused is not allowed any representation. In many cases the only crime these prisoners have committed was speaking their minds. It is not known how many prisoners of conscience there are in Iran at this time, but it is thought that there are many.

A second area of human rights violation cited by Amnesty International is the liberal use of the death penalty. Hundreds of executions are reported every year in Iran, and in some years the numbers are in the thousands (Amnesty International, 1995). No doubt many executions are unreported. The death penalty is used by the Islamic government in Iran for various crimes, including drug-trafficking, adultery, apostasy, and spying. Of great concern is the execution of leaders of non-Moslem religious groups and of opposition political parties.

A third human rights concern is the extralegal execution of Iranians, both inside and outside of Iran. As an example, in 1994 and 1995, four prominent leaders of non-Moslem religions mysteriously disappeared in Iran and were later found dead. All had been critical of the Islamic government at the time of their disappearance and were calling for more religious freedom. Government officials denied any knowledge of these executions, but the circumstances are suspicious.

Iranians outside of Iran are also in danger from extralegal attack and execution. The most well-known case is the *fatwa*, Islamic decree, issued by Ayatollah Khomeini urging the murder of British writer Salman Rushdie for his book **Satanic Verses.** Many Iranians in exile outside of Iran who are critical of the Islamic government have been killed, kidnapped, or harassed. In April 1997, the German court found that the government in Iran had ordered the gangland-style killing of four Iranian émigrés residing in Germany. As a result, the German government expelled four Iranian diplomats from Berlin, setting off an international incident between Iran and Germany. There have been many other attacks and killings of Iranians overseas that point toward the Iranian government, and no doubt many more are unreported.

In summary, Iran's human rights record is poor. Ordinary citizens are arrested and detained, trials are unfair, the accused are not allowed representation, the conditions of the prisons are inhumane, prisoners are tortured, the death penalty is used for many crimes, and Iranians inside and outside of Iran live in fear of "unofficial" attack. Tens of thousands have been executed since the revolution.

How should the world react to these violations of human rights? Is this normal after any revolution, and are the human rights violations any different from Iran under the shah? And, finally, are human rights conditions getting better? It is true that most revolutions bring periods of turmoil in which many people are executed as traitors or reactionaries. And it is also true that there were many human rights violations during the governments of Mohammed Reza Shah and his father before him. Yet these comparisons neither explain nor excuse the present situation in Iran. It still remains that human rights are being violated in Iran on a large scale. But, to be fair, the situation has improved. As in many other aspects of Iranian life, the revolutionary forces are moderating, and the zeal of Islamic fundamentalism is becoming tempered with concerns for human rights. There are certainly fewer human rights violations than there were in the period soon after the revolution, and hopefully this trend will continue.

FOREIGN POLICY: EXPORTING THE REVOLUTION

The Islamic revolution not only changed the internal structure in Iran, but it also fundamentally altered Iran's role in the international community. Before the revolution Iran was an important part of the Western alliance and a firm friend of the United States. In the post–World War II period, the United States, confronted with the threat of the Soviet Union and unfriendly states in the Islamic world, had turned to Iran as one of its major allies in the region. Iran's ties to America before 1979 were strong. The shah visited the United States often, thousands of Iranians studied at American universities, and tens of thousands of Americans lived in Iran as advisors, educators, and businessmen. Shortly before the revolution President Jimmy Carter visited Iran, praising the shah and stressing American–Iranian friendship.

The Islamic revolution completely changed this. The new leaders that came to power in Iran sought to eliminate all traces of American influence, and the revolution itself used slogans against the United States. The Islamic leaders were convinced that the United States had supported the shah and had kept him in power, and were suspicious that at any point after the revolution the United States would intercede to return the shah to power, as it in fact did in 1953. Hatred for the United States grew after the revolution, and by 1980 Washington and Tehran had broken diplomatic relations.

As in many revolutions, the leaders of the Iranian revolution also sought to export their ideology of liberation, in Iran's case Shia Islam, to other Islamic and non-Islamic countries. Many leaders in Iran felt that Iran could be a model for the third world, since it had liberated itself from Western imperialism and from the clutches of the United States. Tehran began to develop a foreign policy based on finding, or establishing, insurgent organizations among communities in countries where Iran felt Shia or other Moslems were being oppressed. Iran soon became involved in creating and supporting resistance organizations in Afghanistan, Iraq, and Lebanon. Afghanistan and Iraq were obvious choices for Iranian intervention. Both countries have sizable Shia communities and border Iran, and in both of the these countries the Shia community is oppressed by the larger society. Iran sent arms and volunteers to both Afghanistan and Iraq and helped train and finance guerrilla movements in these countries. Iran's support of insurgent Shia groups in Iraq played a role in Iraq's invasion of Iran in 1980. Iran was also active in promoting insurgency movements among the Shia communities in the Gulf countries.

Iran became involved in the turmoil in Lebanon as well. Iran has had a long interest in the Shia community in Lebanon, in part because the religious leaders in the Lebanese Shia community trained in Iran and intermarried with Iranian families. Lebanon's leading Shia cleric, Musa As Sadr, was born in Iran and had received his religious training largely in Iran. Iran's opportunity to become involved in Lebanon came with the Israeli invasion of Lebanon in 1982, at which time Iran sent several hundred *pasdaran,* or religious guard, to Lebanon through Syria. These Iranians established guerrilla organizations in the eastern Bekaa Valley, where they proselytized among the poor and homeless. In this way a direct link was developed between Lebanon and Iran that remains to this day.

As with other aspects of Iranian life, Iran's foreign policy has also moderated. Iran is a member of the world community. It belongs to the United Nations, to OPEC, and to other international security organizations. While the zeal of the revolution remains, Iran is clearly becoming more pragmatic in its foreign relations. It now seeks to become a good partner with the other Arab Gulf states. Iran took a nonaggressive stance in the Iraqi invasion of Kuwait and the war that followed, indicating that it is entering a new phase in which anti-Western rhetoric is being replaced by pragmatic actions.

Some may call Iran an outlaw state, and its relations with the United States remain frozen. But Iran has its own grievances and view of the world. Its foreign policy reflects the beliefs and values of the Islamic ideology that brought the revolution to Iran. As these beliefs and values change, so will its foreign policy.

THE TEHRAN SPRING

In May 1997, Mohammed Khatami became the new president in Iran. The size of the vote—he won by over 70 percent—and the policies that attracted such a large following surprised many in Iran and around the world. Although his religious credentials are impeccable—he is a *sayyid*, that is, a direct descendent of the Prophet Mohammed, and the son of a grand *ayatollah*—he won the election with the support of younger Iranians, including women and intellectuals, who were tired of the revolutionary rhetoric and looking for a new, more moderate period in Iran. Khatami promised tolerance in Iran and an end to international isolation. Women began testing the new period by literally letting their hair down. Some in Iran are talking of a "Tehran spring."

Khatami has also taken a bold step by reaching out to the "Great Satan." He has sought a dialogue with the United States, and President Clinton has said he is "very encouraged" (Theodoulou, 1997/1998: 6). In December 1997, Tehran indicated a new attitude of cooperation by hosting an Islamic summit attended by most of the Islamic countries, many of whom recently had been hostile to Iran. Kofi Anon, the Secretary General of the United Nations, attended the conference and came away saying that President Khatami was "a man of his times" ready "to work with the rest of the world" (Theodoulou, 1997/1998: 6).

Part of Iran's new international policy of moderation comes from the sports arena. In early 1998, a US wrestling team visited Iran for a match, the first visit of American athletes since the revolution, and were warmly greeted. More importantly, the Iranian soccer team qualified for the 1998 World Cup, setting off demonstrations in Iran the size and passion of which have not been seen since the revolution of 1979.

Yet President Khatami faces massive opposition from the entrenched political factions that do not want change, including the supreme leader Ayatollah Khamenie, the spiritual heir to Ayatollah Khomeini. The Islamic ideology that fueled the Iranian revolution is still powerful, and distrust of the outside world, especially the United States, remains strong, especially among the old guard. In Chapter 10 we will examine the issues of social change and look at what social change theories predict for Iran's future. It may be too early to speak of a "Tehran spring," but moderation is clearly in the air.

CONCLUSION: THE POLITICAL FUTURE

The politics of Iran have gone through rapid changes over the last two decades. The country's political system has changed from a monarchy to a theocratic republic, and the ruling elite has changed from Western-oriented secularists to Islamic fundamentalists. A new form of theocratic government was created and a new constitution written and ratified. Iran's foreign policy, once closely tied to American interests, has changed to a foreign policy designed to foster revolt and insurrection among oppressed peoples around the world, particularly Shia Moslems. In addition, these sweeping changes have come about as the result of a revolution that has unleashed social and political forces that have a life of their own.

In the last two decades, Iran has been invaded, has suffered terrorist attacks that killed many of its leaders, has had a passenger airliner shot down, and has been the target of international boycotts led primarily by the United States. From Iran's point of view, it is the victim, not the aggressor.

Few countries have undergone such rapid political change in such a short period of time. The presidential elections in 1997 demonstrate that Iran may be moving to yet a new stage of its post-revolutionary evolution. The newly elected president, Mohammed Khatami, won an impressive victory by promising to reform the repressive Iranian lifestyle. His cabinet included the first woman vice president. His election was supported by women, the middle classes, and young people who are looking for a more liberal Iran. Yet the revolutionary zeal has not yet abated, and his reforms are opposed not only by conservatives and hard-liners, but by Islamic radicals in the universities who oppose a softening of the fundamentalist Islamic ideology.

The revolutionary turmoil will continue to buffet Iran in the future. As with all major revolutions, the forces of change once unleashed are difficult to control.

CHAPTER 6

The Iranian Economy

INTRODUCTION

Unlike other parts of Iranian society, the Iranian economy has not changed greatly in structure since the 1979 revolution, despite attempts by the Iranian government to introduce a new Islamic economic model. Although there has been improvement since 1995, the Iranian economy continues to experience high inflation, high unemployment, a lagging industrial sector, a traditional agricultural sector that has failed to modernize, and an overwhelming dependence on oil revenues. In addition, the gap between rich and poor remains, creating hostility among average Iranians.

From the outside, Iran appears wealthy with large deposits of oil and a rich upper class. But from the inside, it is clear that the economy has not developed and that large parts of the economy remain impoverished. Why is this? One sociological approach to economic development, sometimes called **modernization theory,** views economic development as a result of the proper values, attitudes, and norms of the citizens of the country. Economic achievement is thought to derive from attitudes and values that emphasize hard work, savings, efficiency, and enterprise. It is no surprise the industrial revolution developed in England and Northern Europe, modernization theory argues, because the people of this area were hard-working Protestants who valued achievement (Weber, 1974). Underdeveloped societies, as opposed to developed ones, are based on traditional values, modernization theory argues, that emphasize the past, kin relations, ascriptive status, and fatalism; values that do not lead to economic development. Iran's underdeveloped status, modernization theory suggests, is a result of Iran's traditional society and culture in which individual achievement is discouraged and where tradition and kin relations dominate.

Another sociological theory of economic development focuses on a country's position in the **world economic system** (McMichael, 1996). Despite what Iran's officials may try to do to change the direction of the

Iranian economy, or what Iranian attitudes and values may be, Iran's position in this world system determines much of what happens in its economy, this theory argues. The concept of a **world system** was developed by the sociologist Immanuel Wallerstein (1974), who showed that a European-controlled world economic system developed in the 15th and early 16th centuries. This system was originally based on **colonialism,** the system by which the European countries directly controlled other societies for economic gain. In the second half of the 20th century, other mechanisms, such as multinational corporations and economic cartels, have emerged by which the developed countries are able to control underdeveloped countries.

This world economic system has resulted in a modern world in which some countries have obtained great wealth, but other counties have remained poor. The **core** countries, the European countries, and by extension the United States and Japan, make themselves wealthy by exploiting the resources of the **peripheral** countries, which are kept poor, world system theory suggests. The core countries control and limit the economic development in the peripheral countries to keep the peripheral countries from developing and thus competing with the core countries on the world market, and so the core countries can continue to exploit their resources at a low price. As a result, peripheral countries suffer low wages, inefficiency, a large dependence on agriculture, poverty, and high levels of inequality and depend on the export of raw materials to the core countries.

As we shall see, there are limitations to the applicability of both of these theories to Iran. Iran was never a colony, for instance, but the world economy has certainly played a major role in shaping its economic development, particularly in the foreign control of Iran's petroleum industry. Yet Iran's economic development has also been shaped by the unique character of Iranian culture and values and its unique geography. Let us examine more closely the details of Iran's economy.

ECONOMIC OVERVIEW

After several years of slow growth, the Iranian economy is growing more rapidly in most sectors, despite US-imposed trading sanctions. In 1995 and 1996 the gross domestic product (GDP) grew at an annual average slightly above 4 percent (US Department of Energy). The economy, however, has a number of serious problems. Inflation remains high. Consumer prices rose approximately 60 percent in 1995, although the official inflation rate was reported to be down to 35 percent in 1996 (World Fact Book, 1997). In fact, the real inflation rate may be much higher, since the Iranian government enforces an artificially low exchange rate for imports, creating a black market for currency exchange. The Iranian rial, the unit of currency in Iran, is held at an official rate of 1,750 rials to the dollar for imports and 3,000 rials to the dollar for exports. However, the black market rate is closer to 4,000 rials to the dollar and going higher.

High inflation creates enormous social problems. In periods of high inflation, the currency is continually being devalued, and wages of the average citizen are constantly eroding. Inflation also creates a disincentive for saving and an incentive for purchasing, leading to a consumer-driven economy in which people spend their pay as fast as they can before their money becomes worth less. Inflation also makes economic planning, both personal and governmental, difficult.

Iran is also experiencing high unemployment, reported to be 30 percent in 1995 (World Fact Book, 1997). In fact, the real unemployment rate is certainly higher, particularly in some areas of Iran. Ironically, Iran has a shortage of skilled labor, in part because of the continuing "brain drain," as the educated middle class moves to the West, and because of the lack of quality technical education in Iran. Fueling the unemployment problem is rapid population growth. Approximately 600,000 new Iranians enter the job market each year, making the problem of creating enough new job opportunities even more difficult.

Unemployment and underemployment can become serious social problems. Since most of the unemployed are young men, the potential for social and political unrest is great. In addition, problems of crime and increased drug use, which other Moslem countries are also now facing, are becoming major social problems as Iranian youth face an uncertain future.

Iran has also accumulated a massive foreign debt of about $20 billion, partly as a result of financing the war with Iraq, but more from borrowing to rebuild after the war. US sanctions were thought to restrict Iran's ability to repay this debt, but Iran has managed to find medium-range credit from European countries and to reschedule the repayment of at least half of this debt. The foreign debt has greatly restricted Iran's ability to capitalize infrastructure investment. Iran's annual repayment schedule amounts to $4 billion annually and has limited economic development in Iran (US Department of Energy).

OIL

To a large degree the story of the Iranian economy is petroleum. Iran has the fourth largest oil reserves in the world. There is more oil under Iran than in all of the Western countries put together. In addition, Iran ranks second in the world, after Russia, in natural gas reserves. Approximately one-tenth of all of the world's oil and one-fifth of the world's natural gas lie under Iran, most in off-shore deposits (Cordesman and Hashim, 1997). Despite the tremendous wealth in oil, it has only been since 1979 that Iran has had control of its own oil industry. Iran's oil production before 1979 was largely controlled by the British and later the Americans. Starting in 1901, the Qajar government of Iran granted the British a 60-year concession to exploit Iranian oil. This agreement led to the Anglo-Iranian Oil Company, which had complete control over Iranian oil and controlled most of the profits. Although Reza Shah, the ruler of Iran from 1921 to 1941, tried to cancel this agreement in 1936, the British were able to force Iran, through economic sanctions, to sign a new agreement giving them even greater control of Iranian oil.

The control of Iranian oil resources came to a head again in 1951 when the Iranian parliament nationalized the oil industry. Again the British used their might, this time with the help of the Americans, to keep control of Iranian oil. In 1954 the Anglo-Iranian Oil Company created a consortium with a number of American and European oil companies to exploit Iranian oil. Only one-half of the profits went to the National Iranian Oil Company, essentially to the Iranian government, and most decisions regarding drilling, exploration, and refining were made by the foreign partners.

When the revolution came in 1979, the new Iranian government took complete control of oil production and in 1987 passed the Petroleum Act, which gave the National Iranian Oil Company control of all aspects of the oil industry. However, Iranian oil production dropped precipitously after the revolution, from nearly 6,000 barrels per day in the mid-1970s to as low as 1,000 barrels per day in 1979 (Cordesman and Hashim, 1997). This drop was largely because Iran lacked the resources and the trained personnel after the foreign companies left. Iran has slowly been increasing its oil production, but the continued lack of a properly trained workforce and the lack of spare parts have plagued the Iranian oil industry.

Iran is OPEC's second largest oil producer and accounts for about 5 percent of the world's oil output. None of Iran's oil is purchased by the United States, however, which has an embargo on trading with Iran. Most of Iran's oil is purchased by Iran's traditional trading partners, including Germany, France, and Japan (Energy Information Administration, 1997).

Oil is by far Iran's biggest export, producing 80 to 90 percent of its export earnings, followed far behind by carpets (which constitute 40 percent of Iran's nonoil exports), chemicals, pistachios, and metals. In 1996, Iran exported $18 billion worth of oil, or about 3.76 million barrels per day, still considerably less than the pre-revolutionary level (Energy Information Administration, 1997).

Iran's dependency on oil has created an enormous imbalance in the Iranian economic system and has made Iran's economic fortunes dependent on world oil market fluctuations. Self-sufficiency has been one of the major economic goals of the Iranian government, but attempts to develop an indigenous industrial base have lagged behind. Inadequate financing, the lack of skilled labor, and the political misdirection of the Iranian government have restricted the development of a modern industrial base.

THE UNITED STATES TRADE EMBARGOS

Since 1979, the United States has enacted 17 official embargoes or trade sanctions restricting imports to and exports from Iran (Cordesman and Hashim, 1997). The latest trade sanction was signed into law by President Clinton in August 1997. Called the **Iran and Libya Sanctions Act,** this law sought to prohibit all US companies and their subsidiaries from conducting oil business with Iran. This act is part of a larger American policy of "containment" of Iran in response to Iran's support of international terrorism and a concern over Iran's increasing military capability. This latest embargo is also a reaction to the finding that Iran was responsible for the bombing of a US Army barracks in Dhahran, Saudi Arabia, in 1996, killing several American servicemen, and other terrorist acts thought to be sponsored by the Iranian government.

From a political point of view, these sanctions may or may not have had the intended effect on Iran, but from an economic point of view, the sanctions have probably not greatly harmed the Iranian economy. These sanctions have resulted in the halt of some investments in Iran by international companies. The large US-based oil company Conoco halted a $550 million investment in Iran, and other non-U.S. companies, such as Dutch Shell, have decreased prospective dealings in Iran. Iran's oil sales fell briefly as US buyers dropped out and Iran shifted to selling its oil on the spot market. Other buyers, however, have taken the place of the United States, particularly Japan, and Iran's oil revenues were back to normal by the middle of 1997.

AGRICULTURE

Iran has historically been an agricultural country and has vast tracks of land that could be in productive cultivation. The gross value of the agricultural sector reached $25 billion in 1997 (Far, 1997). About 28 percent of the country's workforce is in the agricultural sector, and agricultural exports make up approximately 30 percent of Iran's nonoil exports (Far, 1997). Yet Iran's agricultural output remains low, and Iran must import more than $2 billion worth of foodstuffs annually, particularly wheat, rice, meat, and dairy products, products that it could produce domestically. Approximately 11 percent of Iranian land is under cultivation, and it is estimated that 63 percent of the arable land has not been used, in part because of a shortage of water (Far, 1997). In addition, it is estimated that the land now being farmed is being used at only 50 to 60 percent utility. Therefore, agronomists have calculated that Iran's agricultural output could be seven times higher and that Iran could easily feed itself (Far, 1997).

Agricultural output has increased slowly over the last two decades, but it has not kept up with Iran's rapid population growth. In 1995, agricultural output, for instance, grew at 1 percent, while the population grew at a rate closer to 3 percent. The problems in the agricultural sector of the economy are several, but basically low productivity is a result of the lack of modernization and the continued use of traditional farming techniques. Because of the neglect of the rural areas in Iran, many farmers remain illiterate and unaware of modern farming techniques. Farm plots are small and farming is done with traditional tools such as wooden plows pulled by oxen or donkeys. New seed crops have not been widely adopted, and fertilizers are not widely available or used.

Irrigation is also a major stumbling block in the development of Iranian agriculture. The lack of rainfall has historically restricted farming. However, Iran does have enough water to put many more acres into production if the water could be channeled properly. It is estimated that Iran now uses about 60 million cubic meters of the 135 million cubic meters of water that could be available (Hunter, 1992). The lack of dam building and investment in irrigation works has kept this water from being used.

Despite attempts at land reform and rural development, changing the agricultural sector has proved difficult. Iran's peasants live in thousands of far-flung villages across great distances—many remote. The present government of Iran, and the previous government of the shah, made some effort to bring education to the rural villages and to introduce modern farming techniques. But modernization has been slow to come, in part because of the reluctance of the peasants to accept change, and because of their suspicion of government agents.

In addition, land reform, while perhaps well-intentioned, has not always led to increased agricultural productivity. Beginning in 1963 during the White Revolution, attempts were made to change the land tenure system by taking land from large landowners and giving the land to the tenant farmers. But land reform planners failed to understand that while landlords may play an exploitative role in agriculture by extracting surplus profits, the landlords also play a necessary role in the agricultural sector by providing the capital needed to finance the planting and harvesting of crops. With the landlords removed from the farming process, the tenant farmers were often unable to buy seeds, fertilizer, or equipment, and thus unable to farm the land adequately in any way except by the most primitive methods.

Agricultural policy under the Islamic government is also confused by an ideological split among Islamic clergy over how land ownership should be viewed. Some Islamic theologians believe Islam teaches that land should belong to those who till it, and that land should therefore be given to the tenant farmers regardless of economic consequences. Other Islamic scholars, noting that Islam supports the rights of property owners, are against land reform and believe land should stay in the hands of the landlords. This debate is further complicated by the fact that many Islamic institutions own vast tracts of farmland through the *waqf* endowment system, and are therefore landlords themselves.

Low productivity in agriculture is a continuing problem. Iran should be able to feed itself and even become an agricultural exporter. It has plenty of arable land and enough water, if properly channeled. During the first development plan under the Islamic government, $4.2 billion was spent on agriculture, but so far the results have been disappointing (Far, 1997).

INCOME INEQUALITY AND FALLING WAGES

Over the last half decade, the standard of living in Iran has improved somewhat, but in general, after the Islamic revolution in 1979, the standard of living has fallen or, at best, remained constant. In addition, even before 1979, the gap between the rich and poor was increasing. While the upper and middle classes have prospered, the wages of the working and lower classes have stagnated or declined. At the present time, the major cities of Iran, especially Tehran, have areas of great wealth, with large beautiful homes and fancy cars, abutting urban slums with dilapidated housing, no sanitation or other services, and high rates of unemployment and crime. Some estimates of income inequality in Iran suggest that 90 percent of the total income of the country went to the richest 30 percent of the families in the 1970s (Kavoosi, 1988). In addition to income disparities in the urban areas, there is a large gap between the urban areas and the rural areas, and among regions of Iran.

This income gap has created social tensions and has become the focus of public attention and anger. Income inequality was no doubt part of the motivation for the revolution in 1979, and it is the avowed goal of the Islamic revolution to create an egalitarian and classless society. Helping the lower class—the *mustazefin*, the deprived, in Arabic—was an important ideological goal of the Islamic revolution. Yet, the problems of poverty and unemployment have remained insoluble and, in fact, have become worse since the revolution, particularly in the large cities.

Income inequality can be tackled in two ways. One method is to reduce the income of the rich through high taxes or other methods of expropriation. The other method is to develop programs for the poor to increase employment opportunities and to raise wages. Iran has largely chosen the former. In the period soon after the revolution, income imbalance did decrease, but largely because many of the well-off upper class left, taking their money out of Iran, and property and income was expropriated from the wealthy who stayed. However, living conditions for the poor did not improve. Since the revolution, a new wealthy upper class is emerging, and income disparity is again increasing.

THE ECONOMY AND ISLAM

The teachings of Islam, unlike the teachings of most other religions, include rules and proscriptions regarding economic activity. Islamic scholars speak of an **Islamic economy** based on Islamic rules and principles. These Islamic economic principles include specific policies such as the prohibition on earned interest, rules regarding taxation, and notions of property ownership, as well as more general principles dealing with obligation to community and social responsibility. Like many other topics in Islam, however, there is not complete agreement on many of these tenets, particularly when applying them to a modern economic system. As a result, debates have taken place in Iran over how to create a truly Islamic economy and what that economy should look like.

One issue of some contention, and a basic economic issue, is Islam's position on individual rights to property and wealth, especially wealth generated from profit. An individual's rights to wealth and profit is opposed by those Islamic thinkers who hold that all things belong to God, or to God's representative, the Islamic state. These scholars envision an "Islamic economy" that would have strong control by an Islamic government, a kind of "Islamic socialism." Other Islamic scholars cite Islam's support for private property and refer to sections of the Koran for support. These scholars argue for "Islamic capitalism." Islamic scholars on both sides of this argument can find appropriate references in the teachings of Islam to support their cases.

Historically, Islamic societies have been more capitalistic than socialistic, supporting individual rights to property and profit and creating a capitalist version of an Islamic economy, in which wealth is allowed, even encouraged, and social inequalities are accepted as inevitable. A newer version of an Islamic economy, however, has evolved that focuses on the social responsibility of economic activities in a more socialistic concept of economic good. Some writers have suggested that an ideal Islamic economic system could be described as "capitalism with a social conscience" (Hunter, 1992: 62).

This debate has taken place in Iran over the last two decades, as the Iranian Islamic leadership has tried to sort its way out of the chaos of the revolution to form an economic policy. Many Islamic leaders, especially older members of the clergy, side with the individual rights to profit and property. Historically, many of the clergy were part of the wealthy class and came from families of wealthy industrialists. There is also a strong connection in Iran between the clergy and the bazaar merchants. Many important Islamic clerics are from bazaar families, and the wealthy bazaar merchants played an important political and financial role in the Islamic revolution. Bazaar merchants are the ultimate capitalists, and the clergy are reluctant to anger them. Finally, the "wealth is good" version of an Islamic economy is also supported by many of the Islamic institutions, which hold vast amounts of property from which they generate large profits.

However, the view that an Islamic economy should have a strong social conscience has become a dominant feature of modern Iran. Some members of the Islamic clergy became aware that Islam was growing unpopular with the lower classes in the 1970s and sought to update the image of Islam. As a result, many younger and more radical Islamic clergy in Iran consciously sought to connect Islamic thought with lower-class concerns of social and economic justice. In addition, many of the more militant Islamic scholars were in contact with leftist thinkers during the two decades before the revolution. While the Islamic scholars deplored the antireligious tenets of many of the leftist ideologies, especially Marxism, they did admire the egalitarian goals of those ideologies and the desire for a classless society, which is consistent with elements of Islam that sees all men as equal in the eyes of God.

A new form of ideological Islam began to emerge that combined the egalitarian and anticapitalist tenets of socialism with the religious principles of Islam. Iranian scholars, such as Ali Shariati, who tried to reconcile Islam with socialism became popular. This movement was eventually quashed, and many of its leaders were jailed or killed. Nonetheless, many of the ideas that developed during this period regarding the social consciousness of an Islamic economy still echo in the economic thinking of modern Islam.

Modern Iranian economic policy continues to be pulled by these two opposite forces. The Islamic government is in a dilemma regarding economic policies; it can neither antagonize the capitalist instincts of the powerful bazaar, nor can it abandon the ideological commitment to lower-class welfare. In some ways the shape of the Iranian economy is beyond the control of the government, since revolutionary zeal is still strong among some of the working class. A strong social welfare approach is found in the major industries, in part because of the power of local worker *komitehs* led by revolutionary cadres that have taken over the work floors of the major Iranian industries. Traditional business practices are nearly impossible in the major Iranian industries as worker *komitehs* demand greater participation and benefits. These worker councils and committees have led to greater worker control of factories and industries, but in turn have also led to the flight of capital and managerial and technical talent out of Iran, leaving Iran with a serious talent shortage and the inefficient operation of factories.

The government of Iran has sought to develop its own model of an Islamic economy with an aggressive public sector to provide for the ever-increasing lower class. The latest government plan addresses serious needs in housing, clothing, public health, medical treatment, and education. At the same time, the plan is to do this without weakening an already fragile private industry and services sector.

CONCLUSION

The Iranian economy has a number of serious problems. Inflation and unemployment are high. The nation has a large external debt. Social inequality remains high, and the standard of living has fallen. The Islamic government has attempted to develop an Islamic economy based on Islamic principles. This has led to an economy based on serving the social good, with strong state intervention and control. However, economic problems continue to grow despite aggressive government programs.

Iran's economic situation is also a reflection of its position in the world economic system. Oil continues to dominate the Iranian economy, for better or for worse. Before 1979, the Iranian oil industry was controlled by foreign governments and corporations that extracted huge profits, returning less than half of the revenue to Iran. Now, Iran controls its own oil production, but the foreign countries that departed in 1979 have left Iran with a shortage of trained personnel. In addition, oil revenues are determined by international markets, and fluctuations in world prices have made economic planning difficult.

Once again, Iran is turning to foreign firms to help finance and operate its oil production, despite the US embargoes. A new cycle of foreign dependence may be beginning.

CHAPTER 7

Social Stratification in Modern Iran

INTRODUCTION

One of the significant components of the social structure of any society is its **social stratification system,** the pattern of hierarchical distinctions between groups of people. The story of a society depends much on the nature of the stratification system, how these social distinctions are made, the type and number of tiers in the system, the amount of mobility between these tiers, and the consequences of the social stratification system on the society and the lives of the people. There can be many kinds of social stratification; **slavery** and **caste systems** are two examples often found in pre-industrial societies. In industrial societies, particularly the United States and Europe, the most important social stratification system is based on **social class,** each class being defined as a layer of people in the same or similar relationship to the economy. While there are disagreements among sociologists regarding how to define the social classes, how many there are, or how to measure them, sociologists do know that the life chances one has, including where one lives and goes to school, whom one marries, and in what profession one ends up, depend to a considerable degree on the social class in which one was raised. Further, it is also clear that one's chances of ending up in jail, dying of cancer, becoming mentally ill, or experiencing domestic violence are strongly related to one's social class background.

In Iran, and in Middle Eastern societies in general, social stratification, and particularly the pattern of social classes, is poorly understood and seldom studied. On the surface this seems odd, since social inequality clearly exists in Iran, and in other Middle Eastern societies, and differences in life chances depend on one's social class position as surely as they do in the West. Yet, Iranians, while keenly aware of differences of wealth, power, and prestige, largely deny the relevance of these differences. As a consequence, social scientists studying Iran, with some notable exceptions (Bill, 1972, Zonis, 1971), have not written greatly on the subject.

Social class differences are not often mentioned in the study of Iran or the Middle East for several other reasons. For one, the primary allegiance and identity of most Iranians are to communal groups based on tribal affiliation, kinship, religious sect, or location, rather than to social class. To put it differently, the communal groups to which Iranians generally identify are vertical in composition—meaning that both rich and poor people may belong to the same group—rather than horizontal in composition, as are social classes.

Iranians also tend to deny social class differences because Iranian culture has a strong egalitarian ethos. Poor Iranians believe in their hearts that they are just as good as the rich and the powerful. This egalitarian belief derives in part from the historical importance of pastoral nomadic society and the influence of the pastoral nomadic values on Iranian society. In the pastoral nomadic social structure, decisions are made tribally with the full participation of all adult males in a relatively egalitarian fashion. These societies also have strong codes of manhood that encourage individual valor and bravery. This egalitarian value is also found in Islam, which teaches that all men are equal before God and that the rules and tenets of Islam apply to all men, no matter their station.

Yet social stratification exists in Iran, and Iranians are keenly aware of their position in the social class system, even if they do not acknowledge the system as a whole. Historically, Iranians refer to their society as being divided into three tiers, or *tabagheh,* identified as the upper, middle, and lower classes. In fact, the Iranian class system is greatly more complex. It has roots in the pre-Islamic era, yet is constantly changing with modernization and changes in the Iranian political structure. As with many other elements of Iranian society, there are a traditional class system and a modern class system, both existing simultaneously. In addition, distinctions must be made between urban society, the agricultural society of the rural villages, and the tribal society of the pastoral nomads.

SOCIAL CLASS IN IRAN: THE URBAN SETTING

Upper Class: The Rich Insiders

Iran has historically been an agricultural society, and many Iranians still live in rural villages throughout Iran. However, with some exceptions, the upper class has always lived in the cities. Before 1979, the Iranian upper class was composed of the shah and his court, the members of the royal family; wealthy businessmen, financiers, and industrialists; well-known professionals in law and medicine; and high-ranking military officials. High-level Shia clergy, that is, clergy of the rank of *ayatollah,* had been in this group, but by the late 1960s were no longer considered members of the national elite. The pre-1979 Iranian upper class lived mostly in Tehran, where the royal family lived.

While these people were generally wealthy, the most important determinant of rank among this class was access to power. To be in the upper class, members had to be connected somehow to the power elite. Upper-class members had complex and interlocking relationships within the power structure often achieved and maintained through marriage or kinship ties. At the core of the power structure was the shah and the royal family, including his brothers and sister, who were able to dispense favors and privileges to their confidants, who in turn used these favors and privileges to gain wealth and influence. As Iran industrialized in the 1960s and 1970s, the royal family controlled access to almost every phase of the economic development, from the ownership of corporations to the use of natural resources. During this period, the Iranian upper class became enormously wealthy, essentially by profiting from virtually all of the economic activities of this period.

The families that belonged to this class are sometimes referred to as the "thousand families" (Bill, 1972: 9). This designation is somewhat misleading since there were probably not over 100 families in the upper class at this time, yet the notion that there was a fixed set of families that made up the upper class, and that they had not changed greatly over the years, is correct. Many of the families of the upper class, for instance, were leading Qajar families, or families from previous dynasties, that had managed through intrigue and clever marriages to keep their powerful positions, despite changes in the composition of the power structure. Despite this, however, there was social mobility into and out of the upper class as some families gained in favor while other families dropped out, either through economic ruin or bad marriages. The fluid economic and educational systems of that period also allowed some families to become wealthy through fortuitous investments or success in the modern professions of medicine or academics, and thus work their way into this upper class.

The upper class of that time, from the 1950s through the 1970s, was marked by its opulent lifestyle. Mansions were built in the hills in North Tehran. Mercedes cars crowded the streets of parts of Tehran. Expensive restaurants, shops, and night clubs opened in Tehran, and in other major Iranian cities, catering to the extravagant tastes of the upper class and beyond the means of the average Iranian. Perhaps the most important characteristic of the Iranian upper class of this period was its connection to and identification with a lifestyle that was non-Iranian and non-Islamic. Many of these families had homes and properties in Europe and the United States and spent much of their time living outside of Iran. In addition, many affected Western lifestyles, even while in Iran, including the use of alcohol, Western style parties, and an interest in Western art and culture.

With the coming of the Islamic revolution in 1979, most of this class was swept away. Some stayed, particularly the landowners, financiers, and industrialists whose wealth was tied up in Iran, but most fled, especially those with connections to the royal family or the shah's government. Many had long since transferred their wealth out of Iran and were able to maintain their lifestyle in a new country. Other members of the upper class were less fortunate and found themselves suddenly out of power, out of luck, and out of money. Some of the former upper class were also arrested and tried by revolutionary courts, which often handed out severe punishment, including death.

The New Upper Class

The new upper class is now made up of the top level of the religious clergy and their families, although some of the wealthy businessmen who stayed are reemerging. Since the Islamic revolution, the new upper class is noted by its religious piety. Ostentatious displays of wealth are now discouraged. Yet, the basis of upper-class membership remains the same. Access to power, who knows whom, and the ability to be close to the source of power and to benefit from it are still the prerequisites to being a member of the upper class in Iran. The difference is that before 1979, the core of this power structure was the Mohammed Reza Shah and his family; after 1979 it became Ayatollah Khomeini and his inner circle. After Ayatollah Khomeini's death, upper-class membership has depended on access to the inner circles of the Shia clergy.

The Middle Class

Unlike the upper class, the Iranian middle class has remained largely intact since the Islamic revolution, with some exceptions. The middle class is composed of several distinct social groups, including entrepreneurs, bazaar merchants, professionals, managers of private and public concerns, high-ranking civil servants, teachers, middle-level landowners, military officials, and junior-level religious clergy. While there is only one upper class, there are essentially two middle classes: the new middle class composed of those with a secular, often Western, education and a traditional middle class with close ties to Islam and the Islamic clergy. Members of the new middle class are found in the universities, the professions, and the government bureaucracy. The new middle class is sometimes called the "professional-bureaucratic intelligentsia" (Bill, 1972) or the professional middle class. The traditional middle class is sometimes called the traditional "bourgeoisie" and is made up mostly of bazaar merchants and clergy.

The Bazaar

The bazaar plays important political, economic, and social roles in Iran and is the largest element of the traditional middle class. The bazaar is both a physical place, a marketplace in the center of most Iranian towns, and also a social institution. The urban bazaar is at the heart of all Iranian

Bazaar keeper in his rug shop. Even though the bazaar keepers may appear poor, as a group they play a powerful social, political, and economic role in Iranian society.

towns and cities. It is composed of a series of winding streets or alleyways lined with small shops grouped by product or service. In one area are the carpet shops; in another, all of the spice shops; and in yet another, artisans making brass pots. Because of Iran's hot climate, most of the bazaars are covered. In the smaller provincial towns the bazaar may be a block or two, but in the larger cities of Tehran, Isfahan, and Shiraz the bazaar is composed of a large complex of winding streets that contain not only thousands of shops, but restaurants, baths, mosques, tea houses, and schools. Although the shops in the bazaar appear old fashioned and out of date, it is not unusual to see a traditional bazaar keeper on a cell phone to London, taking orders for oriental rugs, or checking the prices of wool on the world market. Even though the Iranian economy is modernizing, much of the wealth of Iran still runs through the bazaar.

As a political and social institution the bazaar is instinctually conservative and reactionary. Like most businessmen, the bazaar opposes any attempt by the government to impose economic controls or taxation. It is also politically conservative and has opposed the ruling elite through much of the 20th century, especially those who sought to modernize and secularize the country. The Pahlavi shahs viewed the bazaar as a roadblock to modernization and attempted to erode the bazaar's importance. As it had in other political movements, the bazaar played a key role in the 1979 revolution by spearheading strikes and economic shutdowns and by bankrolling the Islamic revolutionary movement. As an institution the bazaar is able to exercise enormous clout—when the bazaar shuts down, the Iranian economy comes to a halt.

The bazaar has consistently been the financial support for the Islamic clergy and helped bankroll the 1979 Islamic revolution. In the post-1979 era, the Islamic government has been cautiously friendly toward the bazaar. However, the government has found it necessary to impose extra taxes and regulations on the bazaar, in part because of the war with Iraq. Like businessmen in all countries, the bazaar merchants have resented the government intrusion into their business dealings, and some tensions between the bazaar and the Iranian government have arisen. The Islamic clergy who now run Iran know, as did the shahs before them, that the bazaar is a powerful political and social force that must be kept happy. The bazaar continues to be the most important and conservative segment of the Iranian traditional middle class.

The New Middle Class

The new middle class is composed, by and large, of salaried professionals working in industry, the government, and the universities. This class is fundamentally different than the traditional middle class, and for that matter all other classes in Iran. The members of the new middle class have generally achieved their position through education and training and are less committed to the traditional power structure that dominates Iranian society. Their class membership is therefore based more on individual achievement and less on ascribed characteristics such as family connection or religious affiliation. The members of the new middle class are also more apt to be oriented toward secular, often Western, lifestyles, in part because of their largely secular education and their international connections. Many were educated outside of Iran, or at Iranian universities that had adopted foreign curriculums and had hired foreign professors. The size of this middle class is proportionally small, but their important positions and visibility make this class important and, when the ideology changes, vulnerable.

After the Islamic revolution a Western education was regarded with suspicion and distrust. As a result, many of those who had gone overseas for their education were required to undergo special Islamic indoctrination courses. Some did, but others refused and lost their jobs. Thousands of Iranians with a Western education fled after the 1979 Islamic revolution, creating a major brain drain in Iran.

The Working Class: Class Insurgency

Like the new middle class, the working class is a relatively new creation in Iran and in the Middle East as a whole. By working class, we refer to the workers in the various industries, factories, and services, mostly created in the last 50 years. By the 1970s a distinct working class identity had developed, and the members of this new class called themselves *kargar*, worker, in Persian. However, the working class has never constituted a unified group. Workers in each industry have their own identity, and the working class is divided into various groups, such as workers in the oil industry, construction, manufacturing, transportation, and mechanics as well as artisans in the bazaar. The most important of these groups are the factory workers, which constituted almost 25 percent of the Iranian workforce by 1979.

Each segment of the working class has its own identity and organization. The artisans in the bazaar, for instance, are organized into guilds. There are internal rivalries within each segment of the working class, in that skilled workers such as plumbers, electricians, and machinists earn higher wages than the less-skilled workers in the same industries and tend to look down on them. Also, many of the lower-skilled jobs are occupied by foreign laborers, primarily Afghans, or workers who have recently migrated to the cities from the rural areas. These workers have the lowest status among the working class and are held in some contempt by the more-skilled workers.

In addition, while the more-skilled members of the working class may do well financially, the less-skilled laborers are generally poorly paid and have neither job security nor benefits. Under both the former government of Mohammed Reza Shah and the present Islamic government, unions have been banned. Strikes led by workers' groups played a major role in the 1979 revolution that brought down the shah's government, but the working class has done no better under the Islamic regime than it did under the shah. The government considers strikes or other work stoppages to be un-Islamic and unpatriotic, and participants are punished.

The Iranian working class has grown in size and will continue to grow as Iran industrializes, despite the efforts of the Islamic regime to slow Western influence. The working class will also grow stronger, as it has in other developing countries, and will eventually have a political voice. However, a history of rivalries and conflict between occupational groups and jealousies and discrimination between skilled and unskilled workers have kept the Iranian working class from becoming organized, and thus it has been easily controlled by whichever government is in power.

The Urban Lower Class

Lower-class members now exist in the poorer areas in all of the Iranian cities. This class has several characteristics: they are unemployed or semi-employed in low-skill jobs; they are largely illiterate; and they live in marginal conditions. They work as street cleaners, small vendors, domestic servants, and in other low-level service jobs. Many only work seasonally or when labor is found. They live in the parts of Iranian cities where there are usually no facilities such as running water or sewers. Their life is difficult, sometimes harsh, and their children generally do not go to school. Many of the lower class also depend on petty theft or begging to get by. At the time of the Islamic revolution in 1979, it was estimated that as much as one-third of the population of Tehran (Metz, 1987) and a quarter of the population of the other major cities were members of the lower class. Lower-class members live on the margin of society, in squalid slums, in poor health and malnutrition, and with poor educational opportunities for their children.

Many of the lower class are recent migrants from the countryside. Because of population pressure or land reform that turned their fields over to large corporations, they have left the agricultural villages where their ancestors worked the fields for centuries. These poor rural immigrants often leave their wives and children in the villages while they come to the cities to look for work. As a result, the urban lower class is heavily populated by unemployed young men.

The Islamic revolution was to be the revolution of the lower class. The Islamic leaders called the lower class the *mostazafin*, an Arabic word meaning the oppressed, and blamed their condition on the government of the shah. The Islamic clergy told them that they were God's people and that their time had come. But in fact their condition has not improved. Many of the lower class were used, sometimes cruelly, in the demonstrations and protests of the revolution, and many became cannon fodder in the bloody war with Iraq. The Islamic government has been slow to offer social services to the slum areas of the cities. Instead it has introduced severe penalties for the petty crimes that occur among the lower class, for instance, making begging a moral offense. The revolution is over, and the poor are still poor.

RURAL SOCIETY

Most of the Iranian population have lived in the countryside until the last few decades. The rural population in 1997 is still estimated to be 40 percent of Iran's population, or about 28 million people (US Bureau of the Census, 1997). Some of these rural folk are pastoral nomads, but most of them are agriculturists, living in over 70,000 villages scattered across Iran. These villages, like villages in other areas of the Middle East, may be very small hamlets of an extended family or two or larger settlements of several thousand. The size of the village depends in great part on the productivity of the land, and consequently on the size of the land holdings, since poor or marginal agricultural lands can support fewer people, while in highly productive areas the villages are larger.

The social stratification system in the rural areas is simpler than in the urban areas. However, the urban class system and the village class system are linked. As in all agricultural societies, the stratification system in the Iranian villages is based on land ownership. The large landlords are therefore the upper class of the villages, but here again it is more complicated than it seems. Only about 50 percent of the villagers own land, and of those, about 75 percent have land holdings below seven hectares, about 17 acres, which is considered too small for anything except subsistence farming (Metz, 1987). Most of the agricultural lands are in fact owned by absentee landlords, including Islamic institutions, who reside in the cities and are generally represented in the village by an agent. These absentee landlords contract with the local farmers to farm their lands for an exchange of a share of the harvest, which can vary from 20 to 80 percent.

The agreement on the sharing of the harvest is based in many areas on a principle of "fifths," which has ancient roots in the Middle East. Growing a crop takes five things: land, seed, labor, draft animals, and water, all in roughly equal proportion. A party receives its share of the harvest according to what it contributes. In this calculation, a landlord that only supplies the land would be entitled to 20 percent, one-fifth, of the harvest. Generally the landlord supplies everything except the labor and, as a result, takes 80 percent of the harvest.

This absentee form of land tenure has some similarities to **feudalism** as it was known in medieval Europe and other countries, particularly in the way in which the villagers, like the medieval peasants in Europe, are forced to stay on the land and in the exploitative nature of the landlord–peasant relationship. Since the Iranian landlords do not live on the land, as they did in medieval Europe, the Iranian form of feudalism has been called **absentee feudalism.** However, there are significant differences between the Iranian land tenure system and the European feudal system. The Iranian system is probably more akin to the sharecropper system found in the American South after the Civil War.

Water is an important issue in farming, since much of Iran is arid or semi-arid. The average rainfall in most of the country is less than 10 inches per year, and in many parts of Iran much less. As a result, irrigation is vitally important for farming in many areas, more so even than land ownership, although it is often the case that the landlord also owns the water rights. As a result, some have referred to the stratification system in rural Iran as **hydraulic feudalism,** meaning those who control the water control the society.

Villages are internally stratified according to who does and who does not own land. The landless villagers include artisans and merchants in the larger villages, but are mostly made up of agricultural laborers. These laborers work seasonally during peak farming periods in planting or harvesting and are paid usually with a share of the harvest. They are without work much of the year.

Each village has a headman, *kadkhuda* in Persian. The *kadkhuda* is not necessarily the most important person in the village—that person is often a clan or tribal elder—but he is the person who represents the village to the local governmental authorities. Historically, the *kadkhuda* was appointed by the landlords, but with the land reforms of the White Revolution during the 1960s, he now is elected by the peasant farmers. However, since he has to demonstrate his access to local governmental officials to get elected, he is de facto appointed by the governmental officials in the nearest town.

While still a large part of the Iranian population, village life is rapidly declining in Iran, and many Iranians have moved to the cities. This change is in part the result of land reform under the shah, which, although well meant, has driven people off the land. It is also the result of the modernization of agriculture, which has brought mechanization and mass-production techniques to Iranian farming. The decline of farming is also a result of Iran's position in the world economic market, in which Iranian farmers were encouraged to switch to cash crops, such as cotton and tobacco, and opium in some places, rather than traditional crops such as wheat or barley for domestic consumption. As a result, Iranian agriculture has become vulnerable to foreign price fluctuations and foreign control and can no longer be counted on for basic subsistence.

The Iranian government has developed programs to help the farmers, but much remains to be done. In the chaos that followed the 1979 revolution, tenant farmers in some areas seized land from the landlords in the name of Islam, and in other areas landlords retook land from peasants that they had lost under the shah's land reform policies, again in the name of Islam. The Islamic government's general position is that Islam teaches that land should belong to those who till it. But the Islamic government has not done much to help the tenant farmers, in part because Islam itself is one of the biggest landlords in Iran.

The position of the villagers in Iran remains difficult. Small plot farming is becoming increasingly problematic and economically untenable. Who can raise a family on 10 acres? The peasants can move to the cities and find work, but they are generally illiterate and unskilled. The cities are crowded with unskilled laborers, and there is little work for them. And the cities are dirty, filthy, unhealthy, and dangerous. The villagers are looked down upon by the urbanites. Their country ways are mocked, and they are the butt of jokes and unkind remarks. They held out great hope for the coming of the Islamic government, but the new government has not been able to solve all of the problems in the rural areas. Their fate is the same as rural migrants in Cairo, Mexico City, and Jakarta. As of now, their prospects are dim.

NOMADIC PASTORALIST: TRIBAL SOCIETY

Pastoral nomads have existed in many parts of the world, but there is no place where they are as important to the social and political development of society as in Iran. While there are no good figures, even today, on how many pastoral nomads there are or have been in Iran, at the turn of the century they may have constituted 25 to 40 percent of the Iranian population. There are about 2 million pastoral nomads in Iran, about 3 percent of the population (Metz, 1987). However, their percent of the population is less important than their impact on Iranian society.

Pastoral nomads live on the slopes of the Elburz and Zagros mountain ranges, but mostly in the Zagros range in southwestern and western Iran. Their economy is based on animal husbandry, primarily sheep and goats. They also have horses and camels for beasts of burden and some cattle, but their real wealth is in their flocks of hardy sheep that they use for meat, wool, and dairy. Their economic niche is quite remarkable. By moving their herds into the high mountains during the hot summers and into the warm plains during the cool months of winter, they are able to survive, and in good years thrive, where permanently settled people could not. However, to do this requires that they make a twice yearly migration into and out of the high mountains during fall and spring, a trip

than can be several hundred miles long. It is the sight of the pastoral nomads migrating with their flocks of hundreds of sheep and goats,
women and children in colorful clothing, and dozens of heavily loaded
camels and donkeys carrying all of their possessions, including pots,
tents, chickens, and sleeping babies, that is perhaps the most enduring
and moving sight in the Middle East.

Despite their ragtag appearance, the tribes have considerable wealth
and power. In a good year the sheep herd can nearly double, and nomadic
pastoralists with large herds can become wealthy. Of course, in bad years
the herds can be decimated. The nomads also wield considerable power in
the Iranian political structure. They are feared by the peasants, whose villages they pass on their migration. Historically, pastoral nomads have
often engaged in the raiding and looting of settled villages. Because of
their hardy nomadic life, the men, and women too, are known to be physically strong, good horsemen, handy with a gun, and courageous.

Their important influence on Iranian society, however, is because of
their cohesive internal social structure, which is referred to as **tribalism.**
A **tribe** is a political or social system based on kinship, real or imagined.
Tribal membership is determined through patrilineal descent, so all the
members of the tribe trace their ancestry to one common male ancestor,
who may have lived many centuries ago. Further, within the tribe, relationships are determined by position in the patrilineal kinship system.
Relationship to other tribal members is determined by their closeness in
the patrilineal descent system. In this way, the closest kin are brothers,
the next closest, male cousins; and then second male cousins, and so on.
This is called a **segmented lineage.** The lineage system holds the tribe to-

*Pastoral nomads move with their flocks of sheep to the high mountains in the summer
months and down into the warm plains in the winter. Their migration may be several
hundred miles in each direction. They must take everything with them, including
children. Despite their ragtag appearance some tribes have considerable wealth and they
have played an important political role in Iran.*

gether, but it can also segment and divide the tribe as well. Subtribes are constantly breaking away from the larger tribe as cousins or even brothers feud over tribal issues. The tribal structure is also relatively egalitarian. There are tribal elders, even chiefs, but most tribal decisions are made in consultation with all of the adult male members of the tribe.

The tribes, therefore, represent an important political force in Iran because of their paramilitary ability and their tight political structure. Throughout Iranian history the pastoral nomads have swept into the cities of Iran to capture the reigns of government. Many of the ruling dynasties began as pastoral nomadic tribes, and important political leaders in recent times have been from pastoral nomadic backgrounds.

Tribes have always been a threat to the national government. During the 1800s, for instance, when the national government was weak, some of the major tribes in Iran, particularly the powerful Qashqai and Bakhtiari tribes, formed a tribal confederation that was essentially autonomous from the central government. It has been the policy of the recent Iranian governments to bring the tribes under control, largely by settling them. Nomads are hard to count and tax. Government officials have always feared that tribal affiliation is stronger than national affiliation, and therefore the tribes cannot always be trusted to do what is best for the national interest.

Tribalism and the nomadic way of life are declining in Iran because of changes in the pattern of land holding in rural Iran. Nomads need large areas of open land for their sheep, but more and more land is being taken up by large agricultural corporations. The shah's government made a concerted effort to settle the tribes, in part by nationalizing the grazing areas.

During the chaos following the Islamic revolution, some tribal members returned, at least temporarily, to the nomadic life. The 1986 Iranian census estimated that there were 1.8 million nomads and about 2.2 million tribal people that had been settled (Metz, 1987). By the mid-1990s the tribes had ceased to be an important factor in Iran. Their migration routes are disappearing, the nomadic way of life is changing, and the powerful tribal families are breaking up. Children of tribal families no longer see the charm of riding a camel several hundred miles each year. Like many traditional parts of Iranian society, tribal nomadic life is vanishing.

CONCLUSION

The Iranian social stratification system is a complex pattern of overlapping, yet separate layers. The traditional class system emphasizes the conservative impulses of the bazaar and the religious clergy, balanced against the role of the royal family and the secular upper class and their desire to modernize Iran. A new middle class of Western-educated professionals has emerged in the last few decades, along with a new working class of laborers in the developing Iranian industries. The rural society is stratified around land ownership, with many of the landowners actually living in distant cities. Tribal society is organized around kinship patterns and an ideology of egalitarianism.

To make matters more complicated, this system has been profoundly transformed by the Islamic revolution of 1979 that swept the old upper class from power and installed a ruling class of its own. Yet the more things change, the more they stay the same. Iranian families still attempt to improve their class position through the strategic marriage of their children. Access to power continues to be the goal of the upper and middle classes, and the poor are still the poor.

CHAPTER 8

Gender In Iran

INTRODUCTION

All societies have expectations regarding the proper behavior and obligations of men and women. Sociologists refer to these as **gender roles.** In America, as in many other countries, these social roles of expected behaviors are changing rapidly as women move into positions formerly thought only appropriate for men. How these roles are defined, and especially how they constrain the opportunities and life chances of women as well as men, are important questions for study in sociology.

Gender roles are defined differently in various countries. What is proper behavior for a woman in a European country may be different from how a woman is expected to behave in the United States. Also, segments within the same country may view things differently; some Americans may prefer that women play traditional roles in the family, while others see women playing an active role in public life, including business and government.

The Moslem Middle East, including Iran, has been called the "patriarchal belt" (Caldwell, 1978), referring to the strong norms of male dominance that exist in the family setting. However, the issue of what is the proper role for women in society is one of great contention in Iran. Should women be constrained from public life and public view and spend their energies raising children, keeping house, and taking care of the men, as the traditionalists who are in power in some Middle East countries argue, or should women be encouraged to participate fully in all areas of society as the equal to men? This chapter will examine these issues, first by looking at the roles of women in the traditional Iranian setting and then by looking at the roles of women in modern Iran. Finally, we look at how women's roles have changed since the Iranian revolution in 1979.

TRADITIONAL GENDER ROLES

The Iranian Islamic revolution in 1979 fundamentally changed the role of women in society by enacting strict rules regarding the behavior of women, including dress codes and what kind of occupations women may enter. Yet, in some ways the revolution simply returned gender roles in Iran to a previous period and, in some parts of Iranian society, reinforced traditional roles that were already in place. Traditional roles for Iranian women are based on two overlapping principles. The first principle, which has been called **classic patriarchy** (Kandiyoti, 1988), defines the proper role of women in society as being in the household, as mothers, daughters, and wives. This role makes women dependent on men. A woman's role in a traditional Iranian family is defined, therefore, by her relationship to men. Her economic security and her primary ties are defined by her relationship to her father, brothers, and, later, husband. She is raised in the family of her father and eventually marries and enters the family of her husband. Later in life she may be known as the mother of some man. Women without male relatives are lost in traditional Iranian society, since they have no status on their own and are scorned.

The second principle involves women's sexuality and defines norms of behavior regarding modesty and virtue. Female modesty in Iran has three components: virginity before marriage, fidelity during marriage, and appropriate public behavior. Codes of appropriate public behavior involve rules for proper dress, the public segregation of the sexes, and such issues as avoiding eye contact or other behaviors that might be construed as flirtatious.

In traditional Iran, men and women who are not close relatives are separated. In addition, women are expected to wear a veil, *chador* in Persian, when in public or in the presence of unrelated males. There are few objects in Iranian life that evoke a stronger reaction from both Iranians and Westerners than the veil. To some the veil is a symbol of "an archaic patriarchal order, an embarrassing relic of the past, and an impediment to development" (Bates and Rassam, 1983: 213). To others the veil represents a fundamental belief in the Islamic faith and the demonstration of proper sexual modesty and morality.

Moslems defend the enforced modesty of women by arguing that in Islamic tradition, the moral and ethical concerns of the community are more important than the rights or comforts of the individual. In this logic, women should cover themselves because it is best for the community, whether they prefer to or not. Contrary to appearances, Moslems believe that humans, including women, are innately sexual and that the sex drives of men and women are strong. In the proper context, that is, in marriage, sexuality is good. However, Moslems also believe that sexuality outside of marriage is problematic for the larger community and that steps must be taken to curb sexual impulses by, among other practices, covering women and segregating the sexes.

This woman is wearing a modern version of the veil, a hoodlike piece of cloth that pulls over the head. She has her body covered with a long loose dress as well. There are several versions of the veil, but they all most do the same job; cover the hair and the shape of the body. This woman is highly educated and a member of the modern professional class.

In addition, veiling has also become a political statement. A woman wearing a veil indicates her alliance to the Islamic movement, whereas not wearing the veil shows her defiance of the current Islamic regime.

Veiling and sexual modesty are also directly related to family honor, and therefore to male concepts of status and manhood. If women violate codes of sexual modesty, the family honor is besmirched, bringing shame to the male elders in the family. As a result, in Iran, a woman's virtue is closely watched by the older males in the family, particularly the father and/or older brothers. Should an unmarried women be caught in a compromising situation, she and the offending male will be punished by the men in her family, for it is their honor that is at stake.

In practice, in the Islamic world veiling can take many forms, depending on the customs of the area and on the degree of modesty sought. In some countries, particularly in the Arabic countries in the Persian Gulf region, women are expected to completely cover their face, body, arms, hands, and feet. In other areas, and among some social classes, a simple head scarf will do, and in many parts of the Middle East no veil at all is worn. Traditional Iranian women wear the *chador*, which literally means "tent" in Persian. The *chador* is nothing more than a large sheet of cloth slightly fitted and long enough to cover the body from the top of the head down to the feet. The *chador* serves two purposes: to disguise the contour of the body and to cover the hair. The hair is considered particularly sensual in Islam. Unlike other parts of the Islamic world, Iranian veils do not cover the faces.

Girls should begin wearing the veil when they enter pubescence, around the ages of eight or nine, but little girls often begin to try to wear the veil at younger ages, in part to act grown up. Iranian women, of course, do not wear the veil in their own homes but only when going out in public or in the presence of men who are not close kin.

GENDER SOCIALIZATION

All societies socialize their members, both men and women, to fulfill the roles that society expects them to play. In other words, all social roles, including gender roles, are learned, and this process of learning takes place from birth to death. In Iran, children are taught early the difference between boys and girls and the proper behaviors for each. Sons are favored over daughters. In traditional society, the birth of a son is celebrated and the birth of a daughter often ignored. Women who give birth to a son are honored; giving birth to a girl is embarrassing. Women who bear no sons are looked down on in Iranian traditional society, and this can be grounds for divorce. The son's circumcision is celebrated, but there is no comparable event for girls. When girls enter puberty and begin to menstruate, it is often met with silence and secrecy.

Little girls are given household tasks and responsibilities at very early ages. Girls at six or seven begin taking care of their younger siblings in the compound, and their behavior is closely watched by the women. Little is expected of the boys. Boys boss their sisters, setting the pattern of male domination at an early age. In traditional homes, especially in the rural areas, when guests arrive, the women and small children must stay in the separate women's quarters, unless the guest is female. When male guests are visiting, the women and small children eat by themselves after first serving the men.

One of the few strategies women have to gain influence and security in a patriarchal system is by forming alliances with males (Kandiyoti, 1988). Iranian mothers form close bonds with their sons that remain throughout life, while young daughters are often closer to their fathers. In general, emotional ties to daughters are not as close as to sons. Daughters will eventually marry and leave to join another family, whereas the son will always be a part of the parents' family. Among the tribes in Iran, there is a saying that sums up this sentiment: "I raise sons for my old age; I raise daughters for someone else's old age."

THE CHANGING ROLES OF WOMEN

By the 1970s the roles of women in Iranian society had begun to change. Women in the educated middle and upper classes of Iranian society had made some progress, and women were found in many new careers outside the traditional family roles. The government of Mohammed Reza Shah and that of his father before him promoted the rights of middle- and upper-class women. As mentioned previously, Reza Shah banned the veiling of women in 1936, and in 1963 his son Mohammed Reza Shah gave women the right to vote. Queen Farah, Mohammed Reza Shah's third wife, was educated in

Europe. She was shown without veil or any head covering in pictures of the royal family and was active in a number of public forums outside the home. The shah's sister, Princess Ashraf Pahlavi, was also an active member of Iranian public life, as were other women of the upper class, and exercised great power in the inner circles of the Iranian power elite.

During the 1960s and 1970s, educational opportunities were increasingly made available for women. By 1976, women constituted 38 percent of the primary school students in Iran, a very high percentage for an Islamic country (Bureau of Women's Affairs, 1995). A number of co-educational universities were established where women attended along with men students. Women entered academic areas, and many women intellectuals joined the faculty of these universities, some achieving administrative positions.

Prior to the Islamic revolution, women also had begun to enter the workforce. Career choices depended in large part on social class position. The middle- and upper-class secularized women in the major urban centers worked outside the home in voluntary charitable causes of various kinds. Others entered the new professions opening up in Iran, such as medicine and teaching. The 1976/77 census showed that 53 percent of the teachers in Iran were women and that 48 percent of the medical students in Iran were women (Bureau of Woman's Affairs, 1995). These two professions were considered especially fit for women in Iran, since they emphasized the female traits of compassion and caring. Women from the upper class also held high government positions during the reign of Mohammed Reza Shah, including cabinet seats.

Among the traditional segment of Iranian society, women largely remained in the home during this period, adhering to Islamic traditions, and only worked outside the home in the case of severe financial need. Many lower-class women were forced to work, especially in the slums of the major cities, because their incomes were needed to support the household. Many women from poor families worked as maids for the Iranian upper-class families or the large foreign community.

Outside the major cities in the agricultural villages, where over half the Iranians lived, the situation in the 1970s was considerably different. The rural people are more traditional and religious than the urbanites, but gender roles are also defined in a more pragmatic way. In the agricultural villages, especially in remoter areas, the veil is less-often worn, and women participate more actively in the work of the village. Villages are generally small, homogeneous places where people tend to know and be related to each other. Villages are often surrounded by a wall, shutting them off from the outside world. Veils are to be worn in the presence of strangers, but in a typical village no one is a stranger, and most people one meets during the day may be related. Also, if women are involved in agricultural work, the veil is a nuisance.

The veil is generally not worn among the nomadic pastoralists, who constitute an important segment of the rural population. While veiling is found among pastoral nomads in some areas of the Middle East, the

Bedouins of the Arabian desert for instance, veiling is simply impractical among the nomads, since women play a very active role in the nomadic economy and each day must milk the sheep and goats, make yogurt, cook dinner, and take care of children, often in a nomadic camp. In addition, during the twice-yearly migration, women must walk or ride many miles each day and then set up camp and do all of the above chores each evening. Clearly, veiling would be impractical for the pastoral nomads.

WOMEN AND THE ISLAMIC GOVERNMENT

Although the separation of the sexes and the veiling of women had certainly declined by the 1970s, at least among some sectors of Iranian society, there were many Iranians, particularly traditional Shia clergy, who found the new changes in women's roles disturbing. To the traditional religious element in Iranian society, women's roles are prescribed by Islam as laid out in the Koran and the teaching of the Prophet Mohammed. Islam says, the Islamic leaders of Iran maintain, that women should stay home, that they should cover themselves when in public, and that the proper role for women is to support the man of the house. In fact, the Koran is clear on some points regarding the role of women but vague on others. Islamic scholars disagree on what Islam says about women's role in society. As an example, the Koran does not mention the veil as such, nor does discussion of the veil appear in the early teachings of Islam. The Koran does say that women should be "modest" in their appearance and that they should cover their hair in public. Some Islamic scholars maintain that the veil as it is now worn did not exist in early Islam but is a cultural leftover from a later historical period, probably Ottoman.

There is a growing feminist movement within Islam that argues that women do have rights in Islam and that present interpretation of Islam is unnecessarily patriarchal (Mernissi, 1987; Fernea, 1985). These Islamic feminists point out that at one time, women played a major role in Islam. As an example, the Prophet Mohammed's first wife, Khadija, was a successful businesswoman in Mecca. She supported the Prophet Mohammed in his ministry and played an important and powerful leadership role in early Islam. The Prophet Mohammed's daughter Fatima was also an important leader in early Islam.

Women were active participants in the 1979 Islamic revolution on all sides of the political spectrum. Many women gave their lives in that struggle. Iranian women had a number of reasons to be angry with the government of Mohammed Reza Shah. Although the educational and economic conditions of some women had improved, many women, and men, in the poorer segments of the society had seen the upper and middle classes become rich, while their lives worsened. Also, economic and educational improvement had not led to increased political participation, and even the middle and upper classes had grown weary of the oppressive nature of the shah's government. As mothers and daughters, many had lost sons or husbands to the shah's secret police. As a result, from the beginning of the

Iranian revolution, women took their places in the marches and demon-strations that eventually brought down the shah's government.

However, as the revolution unfolded, it became clear that the tradi-tionalists had won and a segment of Iranian society led by the Islamic clergy came to control Iran. They wanted to return to traditional women's roles and reverse the trend toward secularization that had taken place in the 1960s and 1970s. Among many modern Iranian women, however, there could be no returning to traditional ways, and they resented the dominance of the traditional clergy. To others the return to traditional gender values was welcomed and enthusiastically embraced. In the new government, controversy grew over rules governing the veiling of women. Instead of the *chador,* the government referred to the covering of women using the Arabic word *hejab,* meaning the modest attire for women, which has a less specific meaning than the word *chador.* The Islamic constitution, ratified in late 1979, enacted a number of rules regarding women's role in society. Many of these rules were controversial. It specified that women should be covered, for instance, but stopped short of insisting that all women wear the *chador,* as some of the more conservative clergy had wanted.

In the chaos that followed the Islamic revolution, the situation of women in public quickly deteriorated. Gangs of Islamic youth, the *basij* in Persian, roamed the streets of Tehran and other major cities on motor-cycles looking for women who were not wearing the veil or who did not appear modest enough. Women found to be out of line were insulted, spat upon, and in some cases stoned or killed. The wearing of makeup, including nail polish, became a sin against Islam, and women who were found with makeup, even if veiled, were forced to wash their faces. In May 1991, the Islamic government announced that it was creating a com-puter data bank of women caught breaking the dress code.

GENDER ROLES IN MODERN IRAN

Even today in Iran, all women out in public, including foreign women, must obey the dress codes. They do not have to wear the *chador* as such but must cover all of the body except the hands, feet, and face and make sure that the outer layer of clothing gives no hint of the body shape. Also makeup and jewelry can be a problem (Javid, 1997).

Men must also obey strict, although more lenient, dress codes. Men cannot wear shorts or short-sleeve shirts. Men should not be clean shaven, although this rule is not enforced for foreign men. Ties are for-bidden since they represent unwanted Western imperialism, although blue jeans are quite common. These dress codes are strongly enforced during the holy months of Ramazan and Moharam.

Public attacks against women regarding restrictive dress codes have forced women in the secular upper and middle classes into a pre-carious existence. While they do not believe in veiling, they find they must do so in public for their own safety and for the safety of their fam-ily. As a modern compromise, many Iranian women now wear a loose full-length dress over trousers or opaque hose and a large head scarf to cover their hair when out in public.

It would be unfair, however, to conclude that the Islamic government in Iran is anti-women and has not promoted women's issues. In comparison to other Middle Eastern countries, Iranian women have done well. The Iranian Islamic government has taken a number of steps to promote women's issues, including women's education, literacy, and maternal health. In the context of the traditional Islamic role of women, progress has been significant. In the political arena, there are 10 women elected to the Iranian parliament, for instance, and two women have been named vice presidents in the government of President Mohammad Khatami. One new vice president is Dr. Massoumeh Ebtekar, formerly known as Niloofar Ebtekar, having changed her first name to Massoumeh, an Islamic Shia saint, after the revolution. She speaks fluent English, having spent part of her childhood in Pennsylvania and having received a diploma from an American high school. She has a PhD in immunology from an Iranian University in Tehran.

The biggest gains for women have come in education, especially in those areas thought appropriate for women, particularly education and health. The participation of young girls in primary and secondary education has increased. In 1993, 47 percent of the children in primary education were girls and 45 percent of the students at the high school level were female (*National Report on Women*, 1995). At the universities, women now account for approximately 30 percent of the students. In some areas, female participation is much higher; for instance, 48 percent of the medical students are women (Bureau of Women's Affairs, 1995). However, only 18 percent of university professors are female, and they are mostly in the lower ranks (Bureau of Women's Affairs, 1995).

In health, the Islamic government has been aggressive in promoting maternal health. The life expectancy for women has increased from 56.7 years in 1979 to 69 years in 1993 (Bureau of Women's Affairs, 1995), and maternal mortality has decreased over the same period from 295 maternal deaths per 100,000 live births to a relatively low number of 54 in 1992 (Bureau of Women's Affairs, 1995). Besides training doctors and nurses, the government has created a local health specialist called a *behvarz*, literally meaning well trained in health issues, in Persian. A *behvarz* is a young man or women selected from a specific region of Iran facing a shortage of health specialists. After two years in basic medical training, the *behvarz* returns to his or her native area to help people in basic health issues. About half of these *behvarz* are women (Bureau of Women's Affairs, 1995). In general, women's health and longevity have increased over the last two decades.

On the economic front, women have not done well under the Islamic government. In 1976, before the Islamic revolution, of the 9.2 million Iranian women over the age of 15, 1.2 million, or about 13.4 percent, were economically active (Bureau of Women's Affairs, 1995). By 1986, this percentage had decreased to 8.9 percent, although it rose slightly in 1991 to

9.6 percent. This decrease in the economic activity of women out of the home in the 1980s and 1990s has been attributed partly to the increased percentage of women in education. Indeed, the statistics show that the major decrease in women working after 1979 occurred in the 15-to-30-year-old category and that women over 30 years old actually increased their economic participation. The decrease in women's economic activities has also been attributed to rapid urbanization, since women in the rural areas are more apt to work outside the home than are women in the cities.

Whatever the changes in educational attendance and urban migration, women have been less active in work out of the home since the Islamic revolution, largely because of the shift in policy toward women's roles in society and appropriate jobs for women. In response to the United Nations' **Decade of the Woman** and the World Conference in Nairobi, Kenya, on **Strategies for the Advancement of Women,** Iran issued a **National Report on Women** in 1995. This report lays out Iran's goals and objectives regarding women's issues and 13 general policies toward the employment of women. These include

1. In the "economic development of women, due consideration must be given to the women's spiritual and material values within the family and the household."

2. "Women's employment in cultural, economic and administrative fields lays the foundation for the achievement of social justice and progress. . ."

3. "Family members [must] subordinate personal prominence to household affairs."

4. Women's employment "must facilitate their spiritual, social, and professional progress and must not exert any detrimental effect on their mental, physical, and spiritual standing."

5. Women should be employed in the following fields: "Teaching, midwifery, and gynecology," as well as "applied, laboratory-based sciences, pharmacy, electronic engineering, social work, translation, and other jobs consistent with women's physical and mental characteristics." On the contrary, jobs in "technical and services sectors" are not recommended for women.

6. "Encouragement of the college educated, specialist women, to assume managerial and executive responsibilities in order to utilize their high-ranking position."

7. Given the importance and the cost of education, women should choose careers carefully and those finishing their education should be assured access to jobs.

8. "The mass media, in connection with women's employment, must follow officially approved policies that effectively block any foreign cultural invasion that stands in contradiction to our Islamic principles."

9. "Equal wages, salaries, and fringe benefits under equal work-ing conditions must be guaranteed for men and women."

10. "Women's employment must guarantee such considerations and advantages as maternity leave with pay before and after giving birth, reduced working hours, social security during un-employment and in sickness, old age, incapacity, etc."

11. "Technical training and vocational training and job opportuni-ties must be provided for women with priorities given to eco-nomically deprived women who are the family income earn-ers."

12. "Suitable in-the-home job opportunities must be created for the housewife-mother who nurture their children."

13. The proper government agencies shall implement the "above-mentioned items and report their achievements to the Supreme Council of Cultural Revolution."*

These 13 policies toward the employment of women in Iran outline the Islamic government's view on women in the workplace, and more generally on women's roles in current Iran. The family is to come first, and women should enter careers that are appropriate to their physical and emotional nature. Beyond those restrictions, however, these princi-ples state that women should receive equal pay and equal working situa-tions. Finally, principle 13 states that the employment of women is being taken seriously at the highest levels of the Iranian government.

CONCLUSION

Gender roles for women in Iran are changing. By the time of the Islamic revolution in 1979, women had begun to play increasingly important roles in Iranian society, although the gains were primarily confined to upper- and middle-class women. The Islamic revolution sought to return women to more traditional roles but continued to encourage women's participation within the traditional framework. Iranian women are gen-erally better off than women in most other Middle East countries. As a whole they are well-educated and experience improving health.

Nonetheless, critics of the Islamic government point out that women in Iran continue to be second-class citizens. How they dress, where they go, and with whom they associate are restricted by govern-ment decree, and their role in society is still defined by their relationship to the males in the population. Patriarchy continues to dominate the soci-ety and the household.

*Source: *National Report on Women*, 1995, pp. 36–37.

Population and Urbanization

INTRODUCTION: THE POPULATION AND THE CITIES

This chapter will discuss two important issues in Iran: changes in the demographic characteristics of the Iranian population and the nature and growth of Iranian cities. In some ways, the Islamic revolution in 1979 was a direct result of social problems created by these two dynamic processes, although their effects were less obvious than the riots and demonstrations that occurred during revolutionary turmoil. The rapid growth of the Iranian population and the movement of people into the major cities created a large pool of unemployed urban poor, mostly young men, whose discontent and anger fueled the 1979 revolution. Rapid population growth and uncontrolled migration to the cities continue to create enormous social problems for Iran.

Iranian cities have a unique character and history, greatly different from the West. While Iran has historically been an agricultural country, the ruling elite have always lived in the cities. Iran's cities are among some of the oldest and most magnificent in the world. The cities have contributed much to Iranian national character. Recently, however, because of shifts in the social and economic balance in Iran, the major cities are flooded with rural peasants, creating large ghettos of unemployed people living in squalid quarters. Tehran, the nation's capital, has grown in size to be one of the world's largest and most densely populated cities. Tehran now dominates Iran politically and socially. Tehran's overcrowding has become Iran's major social problem.

The Iranian population, which was growing rapidly prior to the revolution, has grown even faster since 1979. Iran is now the most populous country in the Middle East, at over 67 million people (US Bureau of the Census, 1997), having surpassed Egypt and Turkey. If it continues to grow at the present rate, 2.6 percent annually, it will have a population over 100 million by the year 2010 and a population greater than 170 million by the year 2050 (US Bureau of the Census, 1997). Why is

Iran's population growing so fast, and what are the consequences for Iranian society? These are the questions to be discussed in this chapter.

POPULATION

The modern study of **demography,** that is, the study of the size and nature of a population, is relatively new to Iran. The first census was conducted in 1956, and population estimates before that are highly unreliable. As in most non-Western countries, even official counts of the Iranian population are probably somewhat inaccurate and unreliable, given the rural composition of the Iranian population and the natural distrust most Iranians have for government officials. After all, the latest US census may have missed several million people. Census data can be unreliable because of two kinds of problems: **coverage errors,** which occur when people are missed, and **content errors,** which occur when people are improperly counted or categorized. Conducting a census in a country such as Iran is difficult since many people live in remote villages or are nomadic, creating coverage errors. Iranians also tend to view government enumerations as preludes to tax increases or conscription into the military and are therefore likely to withhold information, creating content errors. In addition, rural villagers, and many traditional urban dwellers, are illiterate or semi-literate, and reluctant to report women and female children because of Islamic attitudes regarding the seclusion of women. Nevertheless, the broad outline of Iran's population characteristics can be discerned.

Historical estimates show that the size of Iran's population has gone through several stages. The population appears to have grown during the ancient period, reaching a high point in about AD 350. The population of Asia Minor, an area including modern Iran, has been estimated to be about 11.6 million at that time (Beaumont, Blake, and Wagstaff, 1976: 175). From that period until about 1500, the population in this area fell, possibly through pandemics such as the great plagues that went around the world in the 2nd, 6th, and 14th centuries AD. It is thought, however, that the plagues in the Middle East were not as devastating as they were in Europe, partly because of the low population density and the fact that sea trade, by which the disease spread, was less prominent in the Middle East area. The Iranian population also may have declined during the period between AD 350 and AD 1500 because of more or less continuous warfare between Iran and the Byzantine Empire.

By 1500 the population in this area is thought to have been less than six million, a drop of over 50 percent from AD 350, although some estimates (Wilber, 1976: 160) have put Iran's population much higher, especially during the Safavid dynasty. Beginning in about 1500 the Iranian population began to grow again. By 1900 the rate of increase in the population had begun to accelerate, in part because of improvements in farming and health and sanitation changes in Iran.

The first two official censuses of 1956 and 1966 indicated two trends: the population was growing rapidly and the percentage of the population in the rural areas was decreasing as people moved into the cities. In 1956, the first official census showed a population of 18,954,000; in the 1966 census the population had jumped to 25,781,000, a growth of almost 7 million people, or an annual growth rate of 3.1 percent. In 1956, Iran was still predominantly a rural country with over 70 percent of the people living in the countryside. By 1966, the percentage of the population living in rural areas had decreased to 62 percent. By 1986, the last census for which data are available, the Iranian population had passed 50 million and Iran had become an urban country with over 50 percent of the population living in the cities (Iranian Statistical Center, 1995). (The US population became 50 percent urban in the 1920s.) The mid-1996 US Census Bureau population estimates put the Iranian population at slightly over 63 million, with a rural population of 43 percent of the total. From 1956 to 1996, a period of 40 years, the Iranian population has gone from about 19 million to 63 million, and from a country with 70 percent of the people living in the rural areas to only 43 percent. The rural population actually grew in absolute numbers during this period, but its percentage of the total population decreased because the urban population was increasing even faster.

Fertility: Having Children

The major reason for Iran's rapid population increase has been high birth rates. Demographers measure fertility in several different ways. One measure of fertility, called the **crude birth rate,** measures how many children are born each year for every 1,000 people in the population. It is "crude," because it does not take into account the age or sex composition of the population, that is, what percentage of the population are women of child-bearing age. Another fertility measure, called the **total fertility rate,** looks at how many live births an average women would have over her lifetime if she were to bear children throughout her life at the same rates women of all ages were bearing in a particular year. To put Iran's fertility rate into perspective, in 1996 the crude birth rate for the entire world was 24, and the total fertility rate was 3.0, meaning that the average woman in the world would bear 3 children in her lifetime. For Iran the figures are 33 and 4.5, respectively. (See Table 9–1.)

Fertility rates vary considerably by country. For developed nations, which includes most of Europe, the United States, and Japan, the crude birth rate is around 12. For less developed nations, which includes Iran, the crude birth rate is approximately 40. The total fertility rate for developed nations in 1996 was 1.7 live births per women, but 5.5 live births per women in the developing nations (United Nations, 1997). These data show that while developing nations are growing rapidly, women in the developed world are having children at a rate below replacement levels,

TABLE 9-1

Iranian Population Characteristics

Year	Population (millions)	Crude Birth Rate	Total Fertility Rate	Growth Rate (Percent)	Percent Urban
1956	18.9	45	7.5	2.8%	68.6%
1966	25.8	49	7.7	3.0	60.6
1976	33.7	43	6.3	3.1	52.9
1986	49.4	48	7.0	3.7	45.7
1996	63.5	33	4.5	2.6	43.0

Source: Iranian Statistical Center, 1995 and US Census Bureau, 1997.

which is about 2.1 live births per woman. Many developed nations are beginning, or will shortly begin, to experience population declines, unless immigration fills the void.

In Iran, the birth rate has been historically high, by world standards, and high even compared to other developing countries. The crude birth rate for Iran in 1966 was 49 births per thousand, and the total fertility rate indicated that Iranian women at that time would bear 7.7 live births over their lifetime. These rates were among the world's highest, but they had begun to fall by the 1970s. In the 1976 Iranian census, the crude birth rate had fallen to 43 births per thousand and the total fertility rate to 6.3 live births per woman. While still high by world standards, the 1976 fertility rates in Iran showed a significant decrease in childbearing and the beginning of a downward trend.

The falling birth rates in the 1970s were probably linked to several factors that were present in Iran during this period. Iran was rapidly industrializing and people were moving into the cities. Urbanization generally results in lower fertility levels, since it is more expensive to raise children in an urban setting and children are not needed for daily chores as in agricultural families. Fertility rates are also known to vary with modernization and industrialization, so as countries modernize, people have fewer children. Iran was also developing educational opportunities for women during this period, including at the university level. It has been found in other countries that increased educational opportunities for women decreases birthrates, since women tend not to marry and have children as long as they are in school.

In addition, in Iran during the 1960s and 1970s, the government conducted an aggressive advertising and family-planning campaign to persuade prospective parents to have fewer children. The mottoes, "two kids are enough" and "fewer children, better life," appeared on billboards, television, and the sides of buses throughout Iran in the 1970s to attempt to persuade people to limit their fertility. The Iranian government made abortions legal and passed a law in 1973 allowing sterilization. A massive family-planning campaign was initiated in the 1970s to reduce fertility and control the population growth. Studies conducted in 1976–1977, on the eve of the Islamic revolution, show that most Iranian women (85 percent) were aware of contraceptive methods, although only slightly more than one-third (37 percent) had used them. The most popular contraceptive method was the pill, although sterilization was also very common (Aghajanian, 1992).

However, after the Islamic revolution in 1979, the fertility rates again rose. By 1986, the crude birth rate had increased to 48 births per thousand and the total fertility rate to 7.0 births per lifetime for women, very high by world standards in the 1980s. This increase was in part the result of a cultural shift in Iran toward a more pro-natal policy brought on by the attitudes of the new Islamic government. The virtues of marriage and childbearing were extolled on TV and in the schools. All official family-planning efforts ceased, although birth control was not officially banned. In addition, the decade of the 1980s was marked with a very bloody war between Iran and Iraq in which hundreds of thousands of Iranian youth were killed, increasing pressure on families to produce yet more children.

The increase in fertility in the period immediately following the Islamic revolution occurred largely among older women. Generally, older women are those most likely to use contraception, since they have had their children and are therefore past their prime child-bearing years. When contraception was no longer available in Iran, these older women were suddenly at risk of becoming pregnant and began to experience higher rates of fertility. This age-specific increase in fertility may also be because women in this age group had forgone childbearing in the earlier period when family planning and contraception were available. When contraception was no longer available, women in this age group began having the children they had postponed earlier.

By the late 1980s, however, the Iranian government began to realize that the uncontrolled population growth was leading to long-term problems and therefore began to reinstitute family-planning policies and to encourage birth control. In 1989, the Islamic government developed a national family planning program that had three objectives: "To encourage birth spacing intervals of 3–4 years; to discourage pregnancies among women younger than age 18 and older than 35; and to limit family size to three children" (Kalantary, 1992: 1.) To implement this goal, the Iranian parliament passed a series of laws that imposed sanctions on women who had too many children. These laws forbid paid maternity leave for women with four or more children, for example, and forbid government-subsidized day care or health insurance for fourth or higher parity children (Aghajanian, 1992). In addition, the Islamic government reestablished its family-planning clinics and made modern contraception widely available.

As a result of these changes, the fertility rate in Iran began to decline again in the 1990s. The 1996 US Census Bureau statistics show Iran with a crude birth rate of 33, still high by world standards but dramatically down from the 1986 rate of 48. At the current fertility level, an average Iranian woman will have 4.5 live births over her lifetime. More recent data show that the birthrate may be dropping even faster.

In summary, Iran still has a high birth rate, but the rate is beginning to come down. Demographers predict that the birth rate will continue to decrease, and although Iran will grow for the foreseeable future, by the year 2040 the population growth will stop.

Family Planning and Islam

How does Islam in general stand on fertility and family planning? Islamic countries as a whole have fertility levels considerably higher than other countries at comparable economic levels. In a 1988 study by the Population Reference Bureau, it was found that Islamic countries had an average crude birth rate of 42.1 per thousand, while non-Islamic countries at comparable levels of development had an average birth rate of 33.6 per thousand. In terms of total fertility rates, Moslem women around the world have 6.0 children over their lifetime, while women in similar, but non-Islamic, countries had 4.5 children in their lifetime (Weeks, 1988: 13).

Families in Moslem countries are having more children than families of other countries. Is this because Islam is against family planning? The answer is not necessarily. In 1971, Sheikh al-Sharabussi, a leading Islamic cleric at the Islamic university Al-Azhar in Cairo, summed up the Islamic position on birth control by specifying the five conditions under which contraception could be used: when one or both of the couples had a disease that could be passed to the child; when there is a tendency for the wife to become pregnant too rapidly; when there are concerns about the health of the woman; when the man is unable to support more children; and when a man wants to safeguard the beauty of his wife. Certainly most Moslem couples desiring to limit their family size could find that one of these conditions applied. In Iran, Ayatollah Khomeini issued a *fatwa*, an Islamic directive, in 1980, at the very time the birth rate was increasing, approving contraception as long as the mother's and child's health were not harmed.

If Islam is not against birth control, why do Islamic countries, including Iran, have such high fertility levels? The answer, in part, is that Islam takes a strong pro-natal stance. Moslems are encouraged to marry and have children. Having children is seen by many Moslems, especially those in the traditional segments of society, as one way of serving God. In addition, many Moslems, especially those in rural villages or the poor parts of cities, have fatalistic attitudes toward life, believing that the events of their lives are controlled by God—who are they to try to control the number of children they have; it is up to God to decide. This is not an Islamic belief as such, but a traditional life attitude found in many of the lower-class families in Islamic countries.

High birth rates in Islamic societies are also due in part to the role of women in Islam. Women are generally discouraged from working. In most Islamic countries, their normative position should be in the family as a wife and a mother. A woman's prestige in traditional Islamic culture is determined by how many children she has, thus promoting higher fertility rates. Women also tend to marry earlier in Islamic countries. In Islamic countries, the 1988 study found, 35 percent of women between the ages of 15 and 19 had already married, while in non-Islamic countries at comparable levels of economic development, only 19 percent of the women in this age group were married (Weeks, 1988: 21). By marrying at younger ages, Moslem women are beginning their childbearing earlier and will thus have more children over their lifetime. In addition, because of this traditional view of women in society, women in Islamic countries are less likely to attend school, particularly at the university level. Increased women's education is found to be directly related to delayed marriage and childbearing. All of these causes have led to high fertility rates in Islamic nations, and are no doubt a part of the high fertility rates in Iran.

Mortality: Why Do People Die?

The number of people that die in a country depends on several factors. Demographers generally divide causes of death into two categories: **degenerative diseases,** such as heart attack and cancer, and **environmental diseases,** caused by poor sanitation or contamination of the environment. The general health of a population depends on clean water and air, sewage treatment, and other public health issues that reduce the environmental diseases and on modern medical facilities such as hospitals and doctors, which help reduce degenerative diseases. Mortality levels also depend on the age composition of a population. Populations with a high proportion of elderly people, such as in the United States or western Europe, have high death rates, even though health conditions may be good. The elderly are susceptible to degenerative diseases, which are aided more by modern medical facilities and less by public health concerns. On the other hand, countries with a relatively young population will have low death rates, even though health conditions might not be so good, because fewer young people die of degenerative diseases.

Such is the case in Iran. The 1996 estimate for the crude death rate, that is, how many people die each year for every 1,000 people in the population, was reported at 7, one of the lowest in the world! (US Bureau of the Census, 1997). For comparison, the crude death rate in the United States is 9. Are Iranians healthier than Americans? No, just younger. In Iran the life expectancy is 67 years, in the United States it is 76.

A better indicator of the general health of a nation is the **infant mortality rate.** This rate shows how many children die in the first year of life per 1,000 born. The infant mortality rate for Iran in 1997 was 51 (US Bureau of the Census, 1997), not too bad by the standards of developing nations, which is 109, but much higher than the average infant mortality rate in the developed countries, at 11. In the United States, 9 babies die in the first year of life for every 1,000 births. To put this rate into percentages, in Iran about 5 percent of the babies born do not make it to be one year old; in the United States just under 0.9 percent die in the first year of life. Iran has made great improvement in its infant mortality rate, but it still remains above developed countries' standards.

Since children in the first year of life are the most susceptible segment of any population, except for the very old, to environmental diseases, the infant mortality rate is a good indicator of a nation's basic health, sanitation, and nutritional conditions. Because of the lack of vaccines and other medical treatments common in most Western countries, many babies in developing countries die of common diseases such as measles and diphtheria that are no longer problems in the West. The drop in the death rate in Iran in the earlier part of the century, for instance, is attributed mainly to the eradication of malaria, which mostly affected the young.

Many children in the developing world also die of simple dysentery, or of the dehydration that results from dysentery, brought on from drinking unclean water. Many, although not all, Iranian villages have deep wells, but in the newly settled urban slums in Tehran, clean water is not available. In some situations in crowded urban settings, people take their water from ditches or shallow wells where the water is often contaminated from open toilets nearby. This dirty water may not kill an adult, but it does kill children.

The Age Structure: Too Many Kids?

The age structure of the population is generally determined by birth and death rates over an extended period of time. Demographers usually show the age and sex structure of a population in a **population pyramid.** The peculiar shape of the United States's population pyramid is in part caused by a period of high fertility (the baby boom) after a period of low fertility, and then followed by another period of low fertility. The United States's population pyramid, therefore, looks something like a snake that swallowed a rat, and each year that rat moves up the pyramid.

In Iran, like many countries with high birth rates, the population pyramid has a large base and a small top; that is, there are proportionally many more young people than any other age group. In Iran, the 1996 estimates (United Nations Report, 1996) show that 46 percent of the population is under the age of 16. This compares with 22 percent in the United States. This means that almost half the population of Iran in 1996 have been born since the Islamic revolution. Conversely, only 4 percent of the Iranian population is over the age of 65, compared to 13 percent in the

United States. This gives Iran a **dependency ratio,** that is, the ratio of people 65 and older, plus children under the age of 16, compared to the adult population, of 1:1. That is, 50 percent of the population depends on the 50 percent who are adults of working age. This ratio is important, because generally those under 16 or over 65 are not a productive part of the workforce and must depend on others to support them. A high dependency ratio puts a large strain on the resources of the country to support these people outside of the labor force.

A high proportion of young people in the population places other demands on the resources of a country. These young people need to be educated, putting strains on the educational system, and they need jobs and opportunities. Because they do not work, young people create an economic imbalance, so that for each Iranian of working age, there is one Iranian not of working age that the working person must support. Because of its high birth rate and resultant high proportion of young people, Iran is faced with a large population of unemployed and undereducated young people that crowd the poor parts of the cities. They are angry and frustrated, and can become a major disruptive force in Iran's social and political future.

Migration: Who Is Arriving and Who Is Leaving?

Populations also change in size because of in migration and out migration. Iran has experienced both people coming and people leaving in the last two decades, and although the net effect on the population size is about zero, the effects on the country as a whole have been negative. Beginning before the Islamic revolution, but increasing after 1979, a steady stream of educated Iranians have fled Iran for the West. The precise number of people leaving Iran is unknown, since many escaped by sneaking across borders or by being smuggled out of the country. It is estimated that as many as two million Iranians have left Iran for the West, or in some cases, other countries such as Israel or Turkey. The Turkish Minister of Interior, for instance, estimates that there are more than 30,000 Iranians now living in Turkey. There are more than 300,000 Iranians now living in the United States, many in Southern California, which has the largest concentration of Iranians outside of Iran (Hill, 1997)

These emigrants are generally well-educated, many with a modern Western education. Most were members of the former upper or middle class and often were officials of the former government. Many, but not all, have money and were able to get their money out of the country before or after the revolution. These emigrants also include members of religious groups who fear life under an Islamic government, particularly Jews, Baha'is, and Zoroastrians. Most large American cities now have an Iranian refugee community. They are skillful, successful, and well-educated people, and they have been an asset to the communities in which they now live.

To Iran, however, the loss of these educated people has created a serious brain drain. The Iranians who fled the Islamic government were, in many cases, the skilled professionals needed in Iran's development. Iran now has a shortage of engineers, professors, doctors, accountants, and other trained professionals. Their flight has been the West's gain and Iran's loss.

In contrast, there has also been immigration into Iran from bordering countries, primarily Afghanistan and Iraq. The 1986 Iranian census listed 2.6 million foreign refugees in Iran. Of these, 2.3 million were Afghans, and the rest, Iraqis. The Afghan refugees in Iran are in part people who are fleeing the Afghan civil war that has been raging since 1975 (Metz, 1987). The greatest influx of Afghans came when the Soviet army moved into Afghanistan in December 1979. However, many Afghans had also moved to Iran in the 1970s to work in construction in the major Iranian cities, particularly Isfahan and Tehran. Because the border with Afghanistan is largely a barren no-man's-land, Iranian officials are unable to control the movement of Afghans into Iran. Despite its own economic problems, Iran is considerably richer than Afghanistan and draws Afghan laborers, who are often poorly educated.

Iran has attempted to keep the Afghan refugees in camps near the Afghan border, but up to one-third of them are now living in Iranian cities. Most major Iranian cities have an Afghan quarter, usually a squalid part of the old city where the Afghans live in poor conditions. Even though many Afghans speak a dialect of Persian, and Afghanistan was once a part of greater Iran, Iranians look down upon the Afghans as country bumpkins and blame them for many of the social ills, such as theft and drugs.

A number of Iraqis were forced out of Iraq and into Iran during the Iran–Iraq war, 1980 to 1988. Accused of being pro-Iranian or Iranian spies, these Iraqis were predominantly those who lived in the Shi'ite shrine cities of Najaf and Karbala, where Iranian clergy had often traveled as pilgrims and where the Iraqi government suspected Iranian collaboration. Between 1981 and 1982, over 200,000 Iraqis were forced to leave Iraq for Iran. These refugees were accused by Iraq of being Iranians, but in fact most speak no Persian and have no connection with Iran, except for their religious tie to Shi'ism. They have, therefore, had a difficult time in Iran and have settled into poorer areas in the cities of southwestern Iran, particularly Shiraz and Ahvaz.

URBANIZATION

Until the second half of the 20th century, less than 10 percent of Iranians lived in an urban area. Even in the 1990s, the urban population, at about 60 percent, remains proportionately small, especially compared with the West. Iran has been a largely rural agricultural country and remains so to a large degree. Nonetheless, cities have always been important in Iranian society, and an urban lifestyle is a part of the Iranian national character.

The cities are the center of art and literature, the center of religious institutions and the location of great mosques, the home of the country's political elite with great palaces and forts, and the center of Iran's economy with sprawling bazaars. The Iranian cities of Mashad, Isfahan, Shiraz, and Tabriz have played important roles in the country's history and contain beautiful buildings and monuments from the past.

The new urban issue, however, is not the splendor of the past, but the increasing urban blight caused by too rapid urban migration and the lack of municipal services. This problem is not unique to Iran, but is being experienced by almost every developing country and even many of the developed countries. While urban problems are found in all Iranian cities to varying degrees, the largest and most acute urban problems are in the capital city of Tehran, which has grown to enormous size.

Traditional Iranian Cities

Iranian cities are located in Iran according to the geographical features of the country and their functions as trading centers, agricultural centers, or religious centers. The major cities in Iran are located in a loose circle around the central plateau of Iran with location determined in part by the geology of Iran and the availability of water. As Chapter 1 showed, Iran is essentially like a bowl—a central plateau surrounded by mountains or hills. There is rainfall in the mountains, even snow in the winter. But out on the plateau water is scarce—less than four inches of rain per year in many areas, not enough to support agriculture. As a result, Iranian cities have historically been built in a circle on the edge of the plateau, but near the mountains. The settlements must be near the mountains for water, but far enough onto the plateau to find flat land for farming. In some areas, especially in the southern cities of Isfahan and Shiraz, cities are built along rivers that run out of the mountains onto the dry plateau and evaporate.

Iranians have developed an ingenious system of underground water canals, *qanats* in Persian. These underground canals bring water from the mountains out some distance onto the plateau to allow agriculture and human settlement in arid areas that would not support life otherwise. The *qanat* system dates to ancient time. Reports of their use go back at least as far as Alexander the Great in 350 BC, who is said to have marveled at their construction, and then destroyed them. By being underground, the *qanats* avoid the loss of water from evaporation. Their maintenance is tricky and dangerous, however. The men who maintain them, called *muqannis* in Persian, work in the underground canals with a torch and a small shovel, sometimes 100 meters below the surface. Cave-ins are common and many *muqannis* lose their lives each year. Such desert cities as Yazd and Kerman resulted from settlements built at the terminus of *qanats* and still depend on the *qanat* system for water. Before modern piped water, the foreign embassies in Tehran were built at the termini of *qanats*, so as to be guaranteed a water supply in the case of public unrest. This accounts for the fact that the foreign embassies in Tehran are to this day widely scattered around the city.

Many Iranian cities also began as trading centers, located along key trade routes. One leg of the famous silk route that ran from Syria to China passed through Iran, connecting the ancient cities of Nishapur, Rey, Qazvin, and Tabriz. Other major ancient routes include the Royal Achaemenian Road that connected Iran with Greek society in 700 BC. Cities were built along these routes to participate in the economic benefits brought by the caravan trade. As a result, many of the older Iranian cities developed originally as caravansary, a Persian word, and some of the influences of that period can be seen in most Iranian cities still. For instance, the center of most Iranian cities to this day is the large covered bazaar where trade and commerce take place. These bazaars began as central markets around the caravansaries and grew as trade and commerce increased and became more centralized. Many early Iranian cities along the trade routes also had a wall around the inner city, since with caravan trade also came invaders. In many Iranian cities the central fortress can still be seen in the old city, usually near or surrounding the bazaar.

Some Iranian cities, such as Mashad, began as religious shrines. In all Iranian cities, however, religious activities are at the center of the cities. At the core of all the traditional cities in Iran is a large mosque and often a religious school, or *madraseh*, where religious leaders congregate to talk and pray.

Traditional Iranian cities are also noted for the arrangements of close-knit neighborhoods, or *mahalehs* in Persian. Each neighborhood is usually made up of people of similar background or occupation. There is a Jewish neighborhood, for instance; a neighborhood of pot makers; and perhaps a neighborhood of people from a particular village or area of Iran who have migrated to the city or town. The large cities may have many such *mahalehs,* or neighborhoods. The demarcation between neighborhoods is usually not clearly marked, so outsiders may not know they have passed from one *mahaleh* to another. The streets are narrow winding alleyways, so strangers immediately become lost and must ask directions, tipping local people off to their presence.

Each neighborhood has its own organizations, rules, and social institutions. There is often a neighborhood mosque, or place of worship; a local bathhouse; perhaps a teahouse and some small shops; and, in the traditional *mahalehs,* a *zurkhaneh,* or house of strength, where neighborhood men meet to wrestle and perform traditional exercises with large wooden clubs. In the past, these strongmen patrolled the *mahalehs* to protect the local women and keep an eye out for strangers, or others who might cause trouble. These men, sometimes called *lutis* or *pahlevans,* were viewed by some as guardians of traditional values and morals, but by others as reactionary thugs, depending on one's point of view. This role has largely been taken over by the police in modern times, but the idea of neighbors watching after each other still remains.

This traditional *mahaleh* system still exists in all Iranian cities and is an enduring characteristic of Iranian urban life. Like other aspects of Iranian society, the *mahalehs* lack social class segregation. Each neighborhood may contain households of both rich and poor, although the compounds of the rich are much grander than those of the poor. This lack of class segregation is in part because ethnic, occupational, and sectarian ties are more important to Iranians than social class ties. Traditional Iranians would rather live beside those who are like them than beside those of the same class. In addition, families in the *mahalehs* are often closely related and intermarried. Since Iranians depend on kin ties for protection and support, they tend to live in close proximity to relatives.

Within the *mahalehs,* Iranians live in compounds behind high, thick, mud walls. A stranger walking through a neighborhood in the traditional part of an Iranian city will see only high walls, with large wooden doors at periodic intervals. Behind the walls are often lovely family courtyards, with green trees and even a small pool in the center. On the outside of the walls it may be hot and noisy, but in the courtyards on the other side of the wall it is often cool and quiet. The high thick walls not only provide privacy, but they shut out the noise of the city and provide shade from the sun, creating, with the pool and the trees, a kind of microclimate of cool air, pleasant smells, and quietude.

The family lives in rooms arranged around the inside of the walls, leaving the center of the compound open. In the hot areas of Iran, the family lives in the rooms along the wall facing away from the sun in the summer, and, if the winter is cold, in the rooms along the wall facing the sun in the winter. In very hot areas of Iran, which is much of the country, the houses of rich people may contain a tower, or *badgir,* literally wind catcher, that faces toward the prevailing winds. This *badgir* captures the wind; channels it across a pool of water, thus cooling it; and drafts it into the living quarters.

Writers have often commented on the nature of Iranian cities and their living quarters, and the relationship of this to the Iranian personality. In an Iranian city, a stranger sees only the high walls of a hot, dusty, smelly, and noisy city. But behind the walls, where the real people live, it is peaceful, the air is fragrant and cool, and life is good. Likewise, Iranians as people appear to Westerners to be distant, standoffish, and hard to become acquainted with. Yet when they let us into their lives and we get to know them, most are gracious, hospitable, enlightened, and friendly.

The New Iranian City

The traditional neighborhoods continue to exist in most Iranian cities, including Tehran. However, Iran is now experiencing a period of rapid urbanization that is profoundly changing the nature of its cities and overwhelming urban capacity. While this rapid urban growth is happening in all of the cities of Iran to some degree, it is mostly a problem in Tehran. Tehran is a relatively new city by Middle East standards, only about 700 years old, although it is near the site of the ancient city of Rey. Tehran did not become the capital of Iran until 1795. The previous capitals had been Isfahan, Shiraz, and Tabriz. Tehran's rapid growth began in 1925, when the Reza Shah and later his son, Mohammed Reza Shah, centralized government bureaucracy in Tehran. The population of Tehran doubled between 1925 and 1940 and tripled again by the first census in 1956, which listed the population of Tehran at 1.5 million. The city continued to experience uncontrolled growth, reaching slightly over six million in the 1976 census. Data from a 1991 US Bureau of the Census report on the 20 largest urban areas in the world show Tehran as the 16th largest urban area in the world, at about 10 million, only slightly smaller than Jakarta. Tehran, counting the surrounding suburbs, is now thought to be near 12 million in population (US Bureau of the Census, 1995).

The phenomenal growth of Tehran has fundamentally changed the balance among Iranian cities. Historically, but even as late as the 1960s and 1970s, a number of other cities in Iran enjoyed relative importance in the Iranian economic and social life. Isfahan is in some ways the culture center of Iran, a former capital with beautiful old buildings, including mosques and palaces. Mashad has the shrine of Imam Reza where hundreds of thousands of religious pilgrims go annually. Shiraz is the southern city of poets and gardens and an easy lifestyle. Tabriz is the industrial city near Turkey and Azarbaijan. Each of these cities had its own political and social elite, and participated significantly in the national life of the country. Now Tehran dominates Iran politically, culturally, and socially. Nearly one in five Iranians now lives in Tehran.

CONCLUSION

Rapid population growth and urban migration have created massive new problems for Iran. The cities, especially Tehran, are crowded. Many young people are out of work, and the educational institutions are strained beyond their limits. The sanitation services in the urban slums are almost nonexistent, and there is not enough adequate housing. The situation is only becoming worse as rural migrants continue to pour into the city. The Iranian government has tried to cope with these problems and has developed new plans for increased housing, education, and sanitation, but the overurbanization problem is on the verge of overwhelming the country.

Yet, there are signs that the population crisis is abating. If the fertility rates continue to decrease, the Iranian population will eventually level off. Islam does not forbid family planning; in fact, the Islamic leaders of Iran have reintroduced family-planning measures and contraception is now widely available. Hopefully the overpopulation and the overurbanization problems will be solved.

CHAPTER 10

Social Change in Iran

INTRODUCTION

Iran has undergone far-reaching and profound changes since 1979. The government of the shah was replaced by the government of Islam in a revolution of tremendous magnitude and scope. Iran has a new constitution, a new ruling class, and a new ideological foundation. Yet many old problems remain or have grown worse. The cities are overcrowded, the economy is stagnated and too dependent on oil, and unemployment is high. This chapter will look to where Iran might be going in the future by examining some of the major social problems raised in this book and seeing how they might, or might not, be solved.

Social change refers to the variation over time in the nature of a society, including changes in its cultural patterns, its social arrangements, and its basic institutions. At times social change takes place very slowly, so a society may seem to be unchanged to the casual observer over decades or even centuries. At other times, social change takes place much faster, so that within very short periods of time, a whole society may be turned upside down, as happened in Iran. Social revolutions are especially times of rapid social change. The pace of social change appears to be quickening in recent decades in many parts of the world, and the world is much different now than it was only 10 years ago.

In addition, sociologists also know that not all parts of a society change at the same pace, so some segments of a society may be left behind while other segments change more rapidly. This is sometimes called **cultural lag,** and it is generally thought that **material culture,** which includes things such as technology, inventions, and machines, changes more rapidly than **nonmaterial culture,** which includes ideas, attitudes, and values. In Iran, the rapid social change caused by the Islamic revolution has led to a cultural lag, but in Iran's case, between the parts of the society that have embraced the ideas and values of the new Islamic ideology and the segments of Iranian society that have not embraced this new ideology and have therefore been left behind. This split in Iranian society will be a difficult problem for some time to come.

Social change in Iran is also similar to change in much of the rest of the world. Many developing countries, like Iran, are seeking ways to break their dependence on the Western world, both culturally and economically. Many of the countries in the Third World want to become "modern" and economically developed, but to do it in their own style and method, and not to let their culture be swept away by the onslaught of the Westernization. Third World countries in many parts of the world are now seeking to regain their own cultural pride and history. They want economic development, but they do not want to become miniature Americas.

One reaction in many of the Third World countries to the pressure of Westernization has been to return to some form of religious fundamentalism. While fundamentalism is most often associated with Islam, fundamentalist movements have emerged in the last two decades among Hindus in India, Jews in Israel, Christians and Moslems in Europe and the United States, and religious groups in Africa and Asia. This movement represents an attempt to find genuine or traditional cultural values in religious expression and faith, in the face of a changing and confusing modern world. People around the world are looking for something to hold onto in this period of rapid social change, and fundamentalist movements are one way to provide that handhold.

In the Moslem Middle East, Islamic fundamentalist movements have gained enormous power and now control the reigns of government in several countries, including Iran. In some countries, such as Egypt or Algeria, the fundamentalist movement has become an enemy of the government and exists as terrorist guerrilla organizations. In Algeria especially, the Islamic movement has caused enormous death and injury among average citizens. In other countries, the Islamic fundamentalist movement has been embraced by the government and brought into the mainstream of the national political discussion.

At times, the Islamic fundamentalist movement appears oppressive, heavy-handed, and even barbaric to Western eyes. The *Taliban* movement, which now controls most of Afghanistan, has banned, in the name of Islam, almost all women's activities; insists that men not shave; and has even banned kite flying, an Afghan tradition, because the paper used to make kites may have once been a page of the Koran. These prohibitions are considered silly and unnecessary to most other Moslems, who have condemned the Taliban's version of Islamic rule.

However, at its core, Islamic fundamentalism is an attempt to find a genuine cultural basis on which to anchor society and human life. In this rapidly Westernizing world, it is an attempt by the people of Iran to find something that they can hold onto that is theirs. The shah's attempt to Westernize Iran did not provide the answers. In addition, Islamic fundamentalism provides solace for those in the poorer parts of the city, and among those most negatively affected by rapid urbanization and development. Fundamental Islam emphasizes one's duty to family and community; its rules proscribe specifically what is moral behavior and teaches that God will provide. In Islam each person is equal in the eyes of God. These values have sustained many Iranians crowded into the poor parts of Tehran, where there is little work and little hope, aside from religious faith.

The Western world has come to see Islam as a major threat. With the end of the Cold War, the Islamic world has become the new enemy of the West in the minds of many western writers and policy makers. Some writers have suggested that the 21st century will see a clash of civilizations (Huntington, 1996) between the religious and sectarian movements now taking place in the Third World and Western civil society. Yet these divisions do not have to exist. The Islamic government of Iran may seem strange and foreign to us in the West—and it is true that they denigrate the Western world and its values, especially the United States—but they are trying to make sense of a changing world, and to make their own way in this confusing time. No doubt the Iranian government has made many mistakes, but they are their mistakes. If they fail to make a better Iran, it is not for the lack of trying.

CHALLENGES FOR THE FUTURE

As Iran moves into the next century, it faces a number of daunting problems, some of which will assuredly grow worse before they become better. These include urban crowding, a population explosion, a continuing problem with human rights violations, and the role of women in Iranian society. In addition, Iran's role in the world community remains an issue. Let us examine these major problems Iran will face in the next decade and next century.

Urban Crowding

The conditions of the poor parts of the cities are growing increasingly worse as more and more people pour into the urban areas from the countryside. The population of the Tehran metropolitan area is now more than 12 million, and it is one of the most crowded cities in the world. There is little decent housing available in the poorer parts of the city, few job opportunities, poor sanitation, little or no educational facilities for the children, and an increasing drug and crime problem. It is not a pretty picture, and the potential for political unrest grows everyday as people continue to pour in.

On the positive side, there is now governmental awareness of the urban crowding and related problems. The Iranian government is taking steps for the first time to try to deal with them, and now lists poverty eradication and productive employment as two of its top priorities. Iran's new development policies include housing, clothing, public health, and education as major areas to be addressed. It may be that these problems defy short-term solutions, but awareness is the first step on the road to finding answers.

The Population Explosion

Iran's population growth is among the world's highest. At the present growth rate Iran's population will pass 100 million before 2010. The population has already outstripped the ability of Iran's agriculture to support this many people, and Iran must import foodstuffs to feed itself. Population growth creates its own momentum and, as a result, this population problem will assuredly become worse, at least in the short term, before it becomes better.

In addition, the high fertility rate is creating a society disproportionately made up of young people. This high percentage of youth is creating a strain on Iranian resources to provide schooling, recreation, and eventually jobs. For every person in the labor force, there is a person who is too young, or too old, to work that the working person must support. Unemployed and uneducated, some Iranian youth are turning to drugs and crime, a problem other Islamic nations, such as Pakistan, are also facing.

However, the story is not all dismal. Although the population is still growing, the rate of growth is now slowing. The Iranian government has reversed its policy on birth control and is now making contraception available and encouraging family planning. Iranian families are asked to increase the spacing between children and to limit family size to three children. These policies seem to be working, as the birth rate is falling. If the birth rate continues to fall, Iran will have a stable population size by the middle of the next century.

Human Rights

Iran has had a bad human rights record both before and after the 1979 revolution. It has been cited by international groups such as Amnesty International and the UN Commission on Human Rights as a human rights violator. Many political dissenters have been jailed for long periods without trial or hearings, the Iranian prisons are inhumane, prisoners are tortured and generally maltreated, the death penalty is imposed for many crimes, and extralegal harassment and assassinations of critics of the Iranian government have taken place both in Iran and in Europe. These problems can be seen as part of the revolutionary process, but they also occurred during the government of Mohammed Reza Shah.

In contrast, human rights have improved in Iran. In 1990, a bill was passed by the Iranian parliament giving all individuals in civil, penal, and religious court the right to a lawyer of their own choosing. In 1991, the various law enforcement agencies, including the *pasdaran*, or revolutionary guards, were unified and brought under a single command in the Department of Interior to try to curb the revolutionary excesses of some element of the police, particularly the *pasdaran*. As time has passed, the revolutionary passion has cooled and the civil rights violations have decreased.

Women

Iran is a patriarchal society. The traditional roles for women in Iran are defined by Islamic law, which says that a woman's primary place is in the home as mother and wife. Women are defined by their relationship to men. Women's behavior and appearance in public life is restricted and limited. Unrelated men and women should be separated in modern Iran, and women must cover themselves when out in public. In short, women appear to be treated as second-class citizens in Iranian society.

However, Iran also has a number of programs for women and has put the social development of women high on its lists of priorities. Educational opportunities have been made for women, and women students now almost equal men in many fields. Women are encouraged to enter careers where Iranians feel they are best suited, including teaching and medicine. Over 50 percent of the teachers in Iran are female, as are 45 percent of the medical students. In addition, the Iranian government has emphasized maternal health, with the result that maternal death rates have dramatically declined.

Iranians are sensitive to women's issues and resent being criticized by the West. Many Iranians feel that women are more poorly treated in the West than in Iran. While Iran may be criticized for protecting and veiling women, Iranians point out, women in Western societies are actually treated worse. Divorce rates are high in most Western countries, as are domestic violence and other crimes against women. Western women are taken advantage of in pornography and exploited as sex symbols in movie and television in the United States and Europe. From the Iranian point of view, the role of women must be seen in the larger societal context, which includes the good of the community and of the family. The preservation of the family is of top priority in Iran, and women's roles, as well as men's roles, are seen as subservient to that larger goal.

Foreign Policy

In March 1997, a German court ruled that the Iranian government was responsible for the killing of four Iranian émigrés in Germany. The European Union threatened to break contact with Iran, and all 15 European countries withdrew their ambassadors to Tehran. Iran threatened that Germany would pay "high" for its ruling. In 1996, Iran's relations with its neighboring Gulf states deteriorated as Iran failed to return territory it had taken by force earlier. In 1996, Saudi Arabian officials found that Iran was responsible for the al-Khobar Towers bombing at a US military facility in Dhahran, Saudi Arabia, that killed many Americans. Iran's 1997 budget called for a large increase in defense spending, and it has acquired three kilo-class submarines from the former Soviet Union arsenal. Iran remains involved in supporting guerrilla movements in Lebanon and Afghanistan and among the Shia communities in the Persian Gulf states. There is concern in the world community that Iran is attempting to develop nuclear capability through purchases from China and the former Soviet Union.

However, Iran's foreign policy actions are based on its own revolutionary values and concerns. From Iran's point of view, in the last two decades, it has been invaded by a foreign country, Iraq; suffered terrorist attacks on its capital city; and been the target of numerous international embargoes and sanctions, most initiated by the United States. From this point of view, Iran feels its aggressive military position is justified in a world that is out to unfairly punish its actions.

But moderation and pragmatism are now replacing the revolutionary rhetoric and bellicosity, and there is talk of a "Tehran spring." President Mohammed Khatami, elected in the summer of 1997, promised a new, more open era of Iranian international relations. He has said that he will approach the United States with an "open mind." His vice president for the environment, a woman, was raised partially in the United States and speaks fluent American English. Iran is now working with the United Nations on a number of levels and, in general, appears to be seeking to reenter the world community. It has sought to patch up its relations with the other Moslem nations by hosting the Conference of Islamic Nations. In early 1998, a delegation of American wrestlers traveled to Iran for a meet. The American flag was flown and the American team was warmly greeted. In April 1998, a team of Iranian wrestlers came to the United States in a reciprocal move. Time will tell, but it appears that the revolutionary rhetoric is moderating and that Iran is entering a more pragmatic period.

CONCLUSION

Iran has undergone an enormous amount of social change in the last two decades. The Islamic revolution of 1979 turned Iran upside down. Revolutions bring with them strong social forces for change. Many of these forces are good, though some may be bad. Over time these forces moderate and everyday life begins to replace the revolutionary turmoil. More than half of all the people living in Iran were born after the revolution. Post-revolutionary Iran is all they know.

Revolutions also bring to the fore the need for a special kind of leader, or, to use a term from the animal kingdom, *lions*. Revolutionary leaders must be strong and unwavering and demand unquestioning loyalty from their followers. They must have a clear view of where they are going and be able to convince others of the value of that goal. Although their ideologies are different, Ayatollah Khomeini played a role in Iran similar to that of Mao Tse Dung in China and Lenin in Russia. These men were lions.

But sociologists also know that as necessary as these powerful leaders are, a new kind of leader must step forward in the period following a revolution to bring the country back to normal. These men are sometimes called the *foxes*. These new leaders must be more flexible, pragmatic, less ideological, and better at the day-to-day give and take required to run a modern government. The foxes in Iran are just now emerging.

Iran is going through this transition. The old lions of the revolutionary time are giving way to the foxes of the post-revolutionary return to normalcy. All major revolutions go through this process, albeit at different speeds. This transition will take time, but it will happen and is happening. Iran is becoming more moderate and open, and surely will become more so in the future.

REFERENCES

Abrahamian, Ervand. *Iran between Two Revolutions.* Princeton: Princeton University Press, 1982.

———. *The Iranian Mojahedin.* New Haven: Yale University Press, 1992.

Aghajanian, Akbar. "Family Planning and Contraceptive Use in Iran." Paper presented at the annual meeting of the Southern Demographic Association, Charleston, SC, 1992.

Ahmed, Leila. *Women and Gender in Islam: Historical Roots to a Modern Debate.* New Haven: Yale University Press, 1992.

Amnesty International. *Iran: Official Secrecy Hides Continued Repression.* London, 1995.

Anderson, Roy R.; Robert Seibert; and Jon Wagner. *Politics and Change in the Middle East.* Englewood Cliffs, NJ: Prentice Hall, 1987.

Avery, Peter. *Modern Iran.* New York: Praeger, 1965.

Bagheri, B. "A Wedding, Tehran Style." *Persian Outpost* (1997), pp. 1–4.

Bakhash, Shaul. *The Reign of the Ayatollahs.* New York: Basic Books, 1979.

Bates, Daniel, and Amal Rassam. *Peoples and Cultures of the Middle East.* Englewood Cliffs, NJ: Prentice Hall, 1983.

Beaumont, Peter; Gerald Blake; and J. Malcolm Wagstaff. *The Middle East: A Geographical Study.* London: John Wiley & Sons, 1976.

Beck, Lois. *Nomad: A Year in the Life of a Qashqa'i Tribesman in Iran.* Berkeley: University of California Press, 1991.

Bill, James A. *The Politics of Iran.* Columbus, OH: Charles Merrill Publishing, 1972.

———. *The Eagle and the Lion: The Tragedy of American-Iranian Relations.* New Haven: Yale University Press, 1988.

Bozorgmehr, Mehdi. ""Internal Ethnicity: Iranians in Los Angeles." *Sociological Perspectives* 40 (1997), pp. 387–408.

Bureau of Women's Affairs. *National Report on Women.* Tehran: Iranian Government Document, 1995.

Caldwell, J. C. "A Theory of Fertility: From High Plateau to Destabilization." *Population and Development Review* 4 (1978), pp. 553–77.

Cordesman, Anthony N., and Ahmed Hashim. *Iran: Dilemmas of Dual Containment.* Boulder, CO: Westview Press, 1997.

Dupree, Louis. *Afghanistan.* Princeton, NJ: Princeton University Press, 1980.

Durkheim, Emile. *Elementary Forms of Religious Life.* New York: Free Press, 1954.

Eickelman, Dale. *The Middle East: An Anthropological Approach.* Englewood Cliffs, NJ: Prentice Hall, 1989.

Energy Information Administration. *Iran.* Washington, DC: Department of Energy, 1997.

Esposito, John L. *Islam: The Straight Path.* New York: Oxford University Press, 1988.

———. *The Iranian Revolution.* Miami: Florida International University Press, 1990.

Far, B. H. *Iran: An Introduction—Agriculture.* Tokyo: Saitama University, 1997.

Fernea, Elizabeth W., ed. *Women and the Family in the Middle East.* Austin: University of Texas Press, 1985.

Fischer, Michael. *Iran: From Religious Dispute to Revolution.* Cambridge: Harvard University Press, 1980.

Frye, Richard N. *The Heritage of Persia.* London: Weidenfeld and Nicolson, 1962.

Ghirshman, Roman. *The Arts of Ancient Iran.* New York: Golden Press, 1964.

Hill, Jim. "Iranians Feel at Home in US." *CNN Interactive,* May 23, 1997.

Horowitz, Irving Louis. *C. Wright Mills: An American Utopian.* New York: Free Press, 1983.

Hunter, Shireen T. *Iran after Khomeini.* Westport, CT: Praeger, 1992.

Huntington, Samuel. *The Clash of Civilization and the Reordering of the World Order.* New York: Simon and Schuster, 1996.

Iranian Statistical Center. *Iranian Census Data.* Tehran: Iranian Government Publication, 1995.

Javid, Lailee. "A Hat Will Not Do." In *Iran, A Travel Survival Kit,* ed. David Vincent. Victoria, Australia: Lonely Planet Publications, 1992.

Kalantary, I. "Family Planning Program Will Be Established in Iran." *Kayhan International,* January 10, 1991, p. 1.

Kandiyoti, D. "Bargaining with Patriarchy." *Gender and Society* 2 (1988), pp. 274–90.

Kavoosi, Masoud. "The Post-Revolutionary Iranian Economy: Opportunity and Constraints." *Business Economics* 22, no. 2 (1998), p. 35.

Keddie, Nikki R. *Scholars, Saints, and Sufis: Muslim Religious Institutions since 1500.* Berkeley: University of California Press, 1972.

———. "Is There a Middle East." *The International Journal of Middle Eastern Studies* 4 (1973), pp. 255–71.

———. *Roots of Revolution: An Interpretive History of Modern Iran.* New Haven: Yale University Press, 1981.

Kheirabadi, Masoud. *Iranian Cities.* Austin: University of Texas Press, 1991.

Lasswell, H. *Politics: Who Gets What, When, and How.* New York: McGraw-Hill, 1936.

Lipset, Seymour Martin. *American Exceptionalism: A Double-Edged Sword.* New York: W. W. Norton, 1996.

McMichael, Philip. *Development and Social Change: A Global Perspective.* Thousand Oaks, CA: Pine Force Press, 1996.

Mernissi, Fatima. *Beyond the Veil: Male–Female Dynamics in a Modern Muslim Society.* Bloomington: Indiana University Press, 1987.

———. *The Forgotten Queens of Islam.* Trans. Mary J. Lakeland. Minneapolis: University of Minnesota Press, 1997.

Metz, Helen Chapin, ed. *Iran: A Country Study.* Washington, DC: Library of Congress, 1987.

Momeni, Jamshid A., ed. *The Population of Iran.* Shiraz: Pahlavi Population Center, 1977.

Mottahedeh, Roy P. *The Mantel of the Prophet: Religion and Politics in Iran.* New York: Random House, 1986.

Ragin, Charles, and David Zaret. "Theory and Method in Comparative Strategies." *Social Forces* 61 (1983), pp. 731–54.

Roosevelt, Kermit. *Countercoup: The Struggle for Control of Iran.* New York: McGraw-Hill, 1979.

Rubin, Barry. *Paved with Good Intentions: The American Experience in Iran.* New York: Oxford University Press, 1980.

Rypka, Jan. *History of Iranian Literature.* Dordrecht: D. Reidel Publishing Company, 1968.

Savory, R. M., ed. *Introduction to Islamic Civilization.* Cambridge: Cambridge University Press, 1976.

Skocpol, T. *States and Social Revolutions.* New York: Cambridge University Press, 1979.

———. "Rentier State and Shi'a Islam in the Iranian Revolution." *Theory and Society* 11 (1982), pp. 265–83.

Smelser, Neil J. *Comparative Methods in the Social Sciences.* Englewood Cliffs, NJ: Prentice Hall, 1976.

Spooner, Brian. "Do You Speak Persian?" *Penn Language News* 5 (1992), pp. 5, 22–24.

Theodoulou, Michael. "A New Leader's 'Tehran Spring,' " *Maclean's,* December 29, 1997–January 5, 1998, p. 6.

Wallerstein, I. *The Modern World System: Capitalist Agriculture and the Origins of the European World-Economy in the Sixteenth Century.* Orlando: Academic Press, 1974.

Weber, Max. *The Theory of Social and Economic Organization.* Trans. A. M. Henderson and T. Parsons. New York: Free Press, 1947.

———. *The Protestant Ethic and the Spirit of Capitalism.* Trans. T. Parsons. New York: Scribner, 1974.

Weeks, John R. "The Demography of Islamic Nations." *Population Bulletin* 43 (1988), pp. 1–55.

Wickens, G. M. "The Middle East as World Centre of Science and Medicine." In *Introduction to Islamic Civilization,* ed. R. M. Savory, pp. 111–19. Cambridge: Cambridge University Press, 1976.

Wilber, Donald N. *Iran Past and Present.* Princeton: Princeton University Press, 1976.

The World Fact Book. Central Intelligence Agency. Washington, DC, US Government Publication, 1997.

United Nations. *UN World Population Report.* Washington, DC: UN Publication, 1996.

US Bureau of the Census. *International Data Base.* Washington, DC, US Government Publication, 1997.

US Bureau of the Census. *Twenty Largest Urban Areas.* Washington, DC US Government Publication, 1995.

Yarshater, Ehsan. "Loss of 'Persian' Identity Masks Historic Influence." *Persian Heritage* 2 (1997), pp. 15–16.

Zonis, Marvin. *The Political Elite of Iran.* Princeton: Princeton University Press, 1971.

Aba   A loose sleeveless brown cloak worn by the *mujtahid,* or Islamic clergy.

Aghd   Literally "bonding"; the "official" marriage ceremony, usually religious.

Akhund   A general usage term for a religious clergy, usually reserved for local clerics. Once a term of respect, the term now has a slightly pejorative meaning. See *Mullah.*

Arusee   The wedding celebration that follows the *aghd.* This celebration may follow the *aghd,* or official wedding ceremony, by several weeks so the families can raise the money, send out the invitations, and arrange the festivities.

Arya-Mehr   Literally "the light of the Aryans"; used by Mohammed Reza Shah and the shahs before him as a title to indicate their Aryan background.

Ayatollah   Literally "sign of God"; used as a title for the highest level of Islamic Shia clergy.

Ayatollah al-Ozma   The grand *ayatollah. Ayatollahs* who have gained a national following and are judged by their peers to be above the rest are given this title. There are usually less than five or six in all of Iran at any given time.

Badgir   Literally "wind catcher"; this term refers to a high tower attached to houses in the hotter parts of Iran that catches the local breeze and brings it across water to blow cool air into the living quarters.

Basij   Literally "mobilization" in Persian; this term refers to the people's militias that formed after the revolution. The *basij* played an important role in the war with Iraq and were also used to patrol the streets of the major cities looking for Iranians who were not following Islam codes of dress or behavior.

Bazaar   The sprawling central market place in most Iranian towns and cities; often covered. Also refers collectively to the merchants of the bazaar. The bazaar is a strong economic, social, and political force in Iran that tends to be conservative.

Behvarz   A Persian word that literally means "well-trained"; it refers to young men or women who are given training in medicine and public health and who then return to their villages or neighborhoods to work. Developed by the Iranian government to use local people to solve the health problems in Iran.

Chador   Persian word literally meaning "tent"; it refers to the long sheet that Iranian women wear in public to cover the shape of their body and their hair to conform to Islamic rules regarding women's modesty. All women in Iran should cover themselves when going out in public.

Dasht-e Kavir   Salt desert in northeastern Iran.

Dasht-e Lut   Salt desert in eastern Iran.

Dhu al-Hajja   The 10th lunar month of the Islamic calendar, during which Moslems make the pilgrimage to Mecca.

Faqih   Supreme Islamic jurist or scholar; also called the supreme leader of Islamic Revolution.

Farsi   The word for "Persian" in Persian.

Hajj   The annual pilgrimage to Mecca required of all Moslems during the month of Dhu al-Hajja. One of the Five Pillars of Islam.

Hejab   Arabic word that refers to the modest dress required of Islamic women.

Hijra   The emigration of Mohammed in AD 622 from Mecca to Medina, where he established the first Islamic state. This date marks the beginning of the Islamic calendar.

Ibadat   Islamic laws governing religious observances.

Imam   Among Shia Moslems the term refers to one of the legitimate successors to the Prophet Mohammed through the line of Ali. Among Sunni Moslems the term refers to the person who leads the congregational prayers.

Imamzadeh   Literally "son of an Imam"; refers to shrines of the descendants of the *Imams* found throughout Iran.

Jihad   The struggle for the way of God, or the battle for God. In present use, it is often used to mean armed struggle, but in its more general sense it means to do good for God. It is sometimes called the Sixth Pillar of Islam, but it has no official standing.

Jomhuri-e Islami-e Iran   The Islamic Republic of Iran.

Kadkhuda   The elected leader of an Iranian village whose job it is to represent the village to the regional authorities.

Kargar   Persian word for worker. It has become a political term connoting working-class solidarity.

Khutba   A sermon, usually delivered at the Friday noon prayers.

Komiteh   Persian word for "committee"; it refers to local organizations formed after the Islamic revolution to seize control of local power structures.

Luti   A term that sometimes refers to a local strongman who protects a *mahaleh*, or Iranian neighborhood, from strangers or bad people. In contemporary usage the term has come to connote a person of low intelligence.

Madraseh   Islamic seminaries.

Mahaleh   A local neighborhood in Iranian cities. Each *mahaleh* has its own organization and institutions.

Mahriyeh   The amount the groom or his family pays to the bride's family as specified in the marriage contract.

Majlis   The Iranian legislature or parliament.

Maktab   Religious elementary school.

Mashdi   A title for one who has made the pilgrimage to the Shrine of Imam Reza in Mashad.

Masjid   Persian word for *mosque*, an Islamic place of worship.

Minbar   The pulpit in a mosque from which the Friday sermon is given. Usually it is a small flight of stairs at the front of the mosque.

Moharram   The 11th lunar month of the Islamic calendar. On the 10th of Moharram AH 61, Imam Hosein was killed on the Plains of Karbala.

Mojahedin-e Khalq   A leftist guerrilla organization that combined Islamic and left-wing ideology.

Muamalat   Islamic laws governing social relations.

Muezzin   The person who calls the faithful to pray five times each day. The *muezzins* of the past climbed to the top of the minarets five times each day to call the people to pray, but now the call to prayer is done via a sound system.

Mujtahid   Literally "one who exercises *ijtahad*," or interpretive Islamic reasoning. This refers to the highest tier of Islamic clergy or *ulama*.

Mullah   An obsolete term for a local Islamic cleric. Once a term of respect, it now has a slightly pejorative connotation. The more modern term is *akhund*.

Muqannis   Men who maintain the *qanat* system by working in the underground tunnels with small shovels and lanterns. The job is very dangerous.

Mustazefin   Literally the "disinherited"; used by the Islamic clergy in Iran to refer to the poor.

Nabi   A prophet of God.

Namaz   Persian word for *salat*, the official Islamic prayer to be said five times per day. One of the Five Pillars of Islam.

Pahlevan   Literally a "champion"; the term is used for local strongmen who exercise at local clubs called *zurkhaneh*. In traditional times these strongmen protected the local neighborhoods from outsiders. The term now has a pejorative connotation, suggesting a barrelchested oaf, much like the circus strongman in the West.

Pasdaran   Guardians of the Revolution. These groups of men, often young, were organized by Ayatollah Khomeini in 1979 to be the vanguards of the Islamic revolution. They often acted as unofficial gangs of enforcers of Islamic codes and behaviors.

Qanats   An ancient system of underground tunnels used to bring water from the mountains into the desert. Still in use today.

Ramazan   Ramadan in Arabic. The ninth lunar month of the Islamic calendar during which Moslems should fast from sunup to sundown.

Rastakhiz   Literally "resurrection"; the political party created by Mohammed Reza Shah in 1975 to operate a one-party state.

Rasul   A messenger of God, such as Mohammed or Jesus. More important than a prophet of God.

Salat   The Arabic word for the official Islamic prayer to be said five times a day. One of the Five Pillars of Islam.

Sawm   The Arabic word meaning "fasting." Moslems should not eat or drink from sunup to sunset during the holy month of Ramazan. One of the five pillars of Islam.

Sayyid   A title used by descendants of the Prophet Mohammed.

Sazman-e Etelaat va Amniyat-e Keshvar (SAVAK)   Literally the "Organization for State Security and Intelligence"; it was the secret police founded in 1953 under Mohammed Reza Shah.

Shah Nameh   Literally the "Book of Kings"; this is an epic poem written by the Iranian poet Ferdosi around AD 1000 recounting the Persian kings and heroes from the pre-Islamic past.

Shahada   The profession of faith in Islam. One of the Five Pillars of Islam.

Tabagheh   Literally tiers or layers; used to refer to social classes.

Ulama   Islamic scholars or clergy.

Velayat-e faqih   The guardianship of the religious jurist. This is a concept developed by Ayatollah Khomeini and included in the Islamic constitution written in 1979, in which a learned religious clergy would oversee the operations of the government. The first *velayat-e faqih* was Ayatollah Khomeini.

Waqf   Religious endowments, often in the form of land.

Zakat   Arabic word for tithing. One of the Five Pillars of Islam.

GLOSSARY OF SOCIOLOGICAL TERMS

Achieved status   The position of an individual in society that is earned and can change.

Ascribed status   The position of an individual in society that is assigned at birth and cannot be changed.

Authority   Power that is considered legitimate by those who have it and by those controlled by it.

Bilineal descent   Tracing descent through both the male and female line.

Charismatic authority   Power vested in a person because of that person's personality or personal characteristics.

Colonialization   The process by which one country controls another country or society through directed military and political control.

Crude birth rate   The measure of how many children are born each year per 1,000 people in the population.

Cults   Religious groups, usually small and secretive, that start a new religion or break away from an established religion.

Cultural lag   The situation in which one part of the culture does not change as rapidly as other parts of the culture.

Demography   The study of the size and characteristics of a population.

Denominations   An accepted branch of an existing religion.

Dependency ratio   The ratio of people 65 and older, plus children under 16, divided by the adult population.

Ecclesia   A religious organization that claims most members of a society and is recognized as the official religion.

Family   A social contract based on kinship or marriage.

Fertility   The number of children born in a population.

Feudalism   A system of stratification found in agrarian societies in which levels are determined by land ownership.

Gender roles   A set of behaviors considered appropriate for individuals of a specific sex.

Household   An economic or residential unit.

Infant mortality rate   The number of children that die in the first year of life per every 1,000 births in a year.

Legal authority   Power that rests on the legal rules or institutions.

Modernization theory   The theory of social change that describes why some countries become modern and others do not.

Mortality   The number of people dying in a population.

Nuclear family   The husband, wife, and their children.

Patriarchal   The control of women by men.

Patrilineal descent   Tracing descent through the male line.

Patrilocality   The system in which newly married couples live with or near the husband's family.

Patronymic groups   Groups, such as tribes, that are formed and defined by male kinship relations.

Political revolution   Revolution in which the governmental structures are overthrown.

Population pyramid   A chart showing the age and sex distribution of a population.

Power   The ability of a group or individual to control others.

Primogeniture   The rule of descent in which the eldest son inherits the father's position and authority.

Sects   Religious groups that reject the beliefs and practices of the existing religious groups.

Segmented lineage   A system of kin relations that both unites people who are related, but also divides them into opposing subgroups.

Social change   The variation over time in the nature and structure of a society.

Social classes   A system of stratification in which levels are determined by economic criteria.

Social control   A set of rules or understandings that control the behavior of groups or individuals.

Social revolution   Rapid social change in which the government, the class system, and the dominant ideology are overthrown.

Total fertility rate   The number of live births an average women would have over her lifetime if she were to bear children throughout her life at the same rates women of all ages are bearing in a particular year.

Traditional authority   Power that is considered legitimate because of traditional rules, particularly rules of inheritance.

Tribalism   A system of social organization in which social positions and relationships are determined by kin relations.

World system theory   The theory that views the development of a country in its relation to other countries in the world.

INDEX

Child-bearing age, 101
Child-bearing years, 37
Children
 having, 101–104
 number, 106–107
Christians, 10–12, 53
CIA, 26
Cities; *see* New Iranian cities;
 Traditional Iranian cities.
 population, 99–100
Civil servants; *see* High-ranking civil
 servants.
Class; *see* Middle class; New middle
 class; New upper class; Upper class;
 Urban lower class; Working class.
 insurgency, 81–82
Class patriarchy, 90
Clergy, 30, 31, 47; *see also* High-level
 Shia clergy; Islamic clergy; Junior-
 level religious clergy; Shia clergy.
Clinton, President Bill, 65, 70
Close-knit neighborhoods, 110
Colonialism, 68
Comite, 60
Communities; *see* Non-Moslem
 communities.
Compounds, 34–35
Conoco, 71
Constitution (1906), 57, 58
Constitutional restraint, lack, 57–58
Constitutional Revolution, 21–23
Containment, 71
Content errors, 100
Context; *see* Historical context.
Contraception, 103
Control; *see* Social control.
Cordesman, Anthony N., 69, 70, 120
Cossack Brigade, 23
Council of Guardians, 29, 59
Coverage errors, 100
Crude birth rate, 101
Cults, 40
Culture; *see* Indo-European culture;
 Material culture; Nonmaterial
 culture; Pre-Islamic Iranian culture.
Cyrus the Great, 16, 27

D

Dari, 6
Darius the Great, 16

Dasht-e Kavir, 3
Dasht-e Lut, 3
Death, reasons, 105–106
Decade of the Women, 97
Degenerative diseases, 105
Demographics; *see* Arrival; Departure.
Demography, 100
Denominations, 40
Departure, demographics, 107–108
Dependency ratio, 107
Dhu al-Hajja, 46
Dialects, 6
Diseases; *see* Degenerative diseases;
 Environmental diseases.
Dissent; *see* Political dissent.
Dupree, Louis, 120
Durkheim, Emile, 40, 120
Dutch Shell, 71

E

Ecclesia, 40
Economic development; *see* Women.
Economic overview, 68–69
Economic system; *see* World economic
 system.
Economy; *see* Iranian economy; Islamic
 economy.
 Islam, 73–75
Eickelman, Dale, 120
Elamites, 16
Embargo; *see* United States trade
 embargo.
Endowments, 49, 52
Energy Information Administration,
 70, 120
Environment, 1–14
 conclusion, 13–14
 introduction, 1–2
Environmental diseases, 105
Errors; *see* Content errors; Coverage
 errors.
Esposito, John L., 43, 45, 120
Ethno-linguistic groups, 7, 13–14
European Union, 117
European-controlled world economic
 system, 68
Extended families, 34–35